Meet Me at the Cross

Ginny Emery, Editor

Joyce Long, Editor

Janet Emery, Art Editor

Tom Adams, Typography

Jeane Heckert, Page Layout & Design

Maria Johnson, Copy Editor

Joyce Pfitzinger, Compilation

Meet Me at the Cross

Given Word Publishers   Crystal Lake, Illinois

2000

Cover drawing: Janet Emery

"Come unto Me" and "Repentance" from *Heart Songs,* a collection of Poems and Meditations by Pat Bailey, © Pat Bailey, 1998. Used by permission.

"What Can I Offer" by Bob Baker and "All I Can Do" by Steve Curtis, © Kerygma Music, 1998. Used by permission.

Photographs from ballet, line drawings of worshippers, and *Worshipping into the Heart of God* by Diane Wawrejko Cochrane, © Dances Wawrejko. Used by permission.

"A Huge Lesson" and "Putting all our Expectancies in the Blood of the Cross" were transcribed and adapted from teachings by C. S. Kellough. Used by permission.

"The Blood that Covers Me" by Mark Oliver, © Mighty Warrior Music ULTD, 1998. Used by permission.

Jesus Laughing is a colored variation of Willis Wheatley's drawing by Ralph Kozak,© 1997 Praise Screen Prints, 10485 S. Mt. Josh Dr., Traverse City, MI Phone: 616-941-4880. Used by permission.

Grateful acknowledgment is made to Master's Prints, P. O. Box 1015; Jenison, MI 49429 for permission to use "Our Father," a pencil drawing by Jeffrey Scott Terpstra.

Grateful acknowledgment is made to Word Publishing for permission to quote from *Can Man Live Without God,* Ravi Zacharias, 1994, Word Publishing, Nashville, TN. All rights reserved.

All scripture quotations, unless otherwise indicated, are taken from the HOLY BIBLE, NEW INTERNATIONAL VERSION®. NIV®. Copyright © 1973, 1978, 1984 by International Bible Society. Used by permission of Zondervan Publishing House. All rights reserved.

Scripture quotations marked (AMP) taken from the *Amplified Bible, Old Testament*, Copyright © 1965, 1987 by the Zondervan Corporation. The Amplified New Testament, Copyright © 1954, 1958, 1987 by the The Lockman Foundation. Used by permission.

Scripture quotations marked (NASB) taken from the NEW AMERICAN STANDARD BIBLE®, Copyright © The Lockman Foundation 1960, 1962, 1963, 1968, 1971, 1972, 1973, 1975, 1977, Used by permission.

Scripture quotations marked (NKJV) are taken from the New King James Version. Copyright © 1982 by Thomas Nelson, Inc. Used by permission. All rights reserved.

Scripture quotations marked (NLT) are taken from the Holy Bible, *New Living Translation,* Copyright © 1996. Used by permission of Tyndale House Publishers, Inc., Wheaton, Illinois 60189. All rights reserved.

Although every effort has been made to ensure the accuracy of this book, we assume no responsibility for errors, inaccuracies, omissions, or any inconsistency herein. Any slights of people, places, or organizations are unintentional.

MEET ME AT THE CROSS, 1999, Ginny Ann Emery and Joyce Long, Editors
Printed and bound in the United States of America

First Printing

ISBN: 0-9676193-1-9

This book is a gift to the body of Christ. To extend the Kingdom of God, you may reproduce all non-copyrighted materials except those used by permission. Please do NOT reproduce this book or any portion of it for financial gain. Profits from the sale of this book by GIVEN WORD PUBLISHERS, Inc. will be used to extend the Kingdom of God.

ACKNOWLEDGMENTS

No printed words can capture our wonder before God or the gratitude we want to express to everyone who shared his/her life at the cross in pictures, words, and labor for this book. We celebrate the contributors by listing their names at the back of the book. No one was paid; everyone gave freely. Each person helped us to see and understand another part of what Jesus actually accomplished at the cross.

Many others helped bring the book to completion. Thank you to Ed, Bill, Tom, Dan, Anne, Sue, Lori, Maria, Karen, Joyce, Mary, Helen, Judy, Jen, Kathleen, Alice, the Wednesday morning prayer group, and all the others who believed in it.

Seeds only grow in fertile soil. The idea for *Meet Me at the Cross* grew in the good soil of The Vineyard Christian Fellowship of Elgin, Illinois.

Special words of thanksgiving go to Tom Adams who guided the typesetting, Jeane Heckert for page layout and design, and Joyce Pfitzinger for helping to compile contributions. Lori Hall's prayers kept the book alive when it was near death, and Maria Johnson provided encouragement, insight and editing. Janet Emery gave artistic oversight in details and in wonderful drawings. Patricia Repp helped with proofreading. Finally, Rinck Heule and his team at PrintSystems, Inc. added the professional finishing touches that transformed our work into this volume.

As we joined together, a living word of faith sprang forth among us. God died for us all, yet He reveals His cross to us as individuals, separate and alone (John 17:21). When we choose to behold His glory together, He blesses us with previously hidden dimensions of Himself. Inevitably, whenever we turn to face Him at the cross, we are humbled by the depths of His love.

Blessings,
Ginny Emery and Joyce Long

Note: Our intent is devotional not doctrinal. We are ordinary believers, not theologians. We want to see Jesus—to love and adore Him. Pictures, poetry, and persuasion may be passionately one-sided. Scriptures are given for illustrative and devotional use. Please do not look for balanced theology that will resolve the paradoxes and mysteries of faith. The scriptures are not meant to be used for justification of or doctrinal support for the writings and pictures they accompany.

Contents

	Introduction	*8*
	Foreword	*11*
1	*The Pain of Separation*	*13*
2	*Love's Answer is Redemption*	*35*
3	*Union with Him*	*75*
	Afterword	*150*
	Index of Contributions	*152*
	The Writers	*154*
	The Artists	*156*
	Resources	*158*

INTRODUCTION

The cross is the strongest symbol of Christian faith. In A.D. 33, Jesus from Nazareth, the Son of God and a totally innocent man, was crucified. His life and death fulfilled prophecies made hundreds of years before His birth. He was buried and three days later, He rose from the dead. The historical facts about Jesus' death, burial, and resurrection do not begin to explain the meaning of His death on the cross.

The power released through faith in Jesus' redemptive suffering and death on the cross is one of the mysteries of Christianity. The human mind cannot fathom it. Only the Holy Spirit of God Himself can take us to the cross and teach us its wisdom. As Paul wrote in First Corinthians 1:18 and 19: The message of the cross is foolishness to those who are perishing, but to us who are being saved, it is the power of God. For it is written:

I will destroy the wisdom of the wise,
the intelligence of the intelligent I will frustrate.

Jesus calls us to the cross whenever God's ways collide with man's ways. When, in His plan, we don't get what we want and everything seems (humanly speaking) to be going awry, we need to meet with Him at Calvary and walk through the cross into His resurrection life.

MEET ME AT THE CROSS began with a few poems. It grew as a love offering to Jesus—for those who fear the Lord speak to one another (Malachi 3:16). Friends, many from the Elgin Vineyard Christian Fellowship, and others whose lives fed into the Elgin family, shared their understanding and experiences of the cross. Surprising us, words from one person fit pictures from another as if bone were being fit to bone, joint to joint (Ezekiel 37).

Selections in this book are diverse, yet unified. Some contributions are artistically excellent; others are less skillful. Nothing was included for its artistic merit alone; everything points to the cross and the Life blood given there. This work includes preaching, teaching, pictures, poetry, song, journal excerpts, and testimonies. Contributors range from seasoned older pastors to new believers and children. There are words of understanding and truth, worship and adoration, gratitude and praise, as well as cries of contrition, repentance, longing and need—a need to meet with one another and with Jesus at the foot of the cross.

God the Father sent Jesus to the cross; God the Son chose to die on the cross; and God the Holy Spirit opens our eyes to the truth of their powerful affection for us. When we see the cross from their perspective, we know that we are loved.

† † †

In A.D. 33
JESUS from NAZARETH,
the Son of God,
a totally innocent man,
was crucified.

FOREWORD

There is a tremendous need today for a book like the one you hold in your hands, a book that calls us to the cross. The Apostle Paul wrote that he "determined not to know anything among you except Jesus Christ and Him crucified" (1 Cor. 2:2 NKJV).

I know this simplicity of focus was the door to life for Paul and it remains the door to life for us as well.

Let's meet Him at the cross!

Thomas Severson
Pastor, Vineyard Christian Fellowship,
Elgin, Illinois

1 The Pain of Separation

Who shall separate us from the love of Christ?
Shall trouble or hardship or persecution
or famine or nakedness or danger or sword?

Romans 8:35

God's Revelation
of His Purpose
and of His Love for man
centers in the cross

It
begins
in creation

CREATION *Abigail Apon, age 10*

With a twinkle in God's eye,
The stars were in the sky!
With a sunshiny look on His face,
He made the light and sun with thought and grace.

Then He reached into the air
And grabbed onto nothing.
He molded it round and then He had something!

He reached into the earth and made a small mound,
And ants came crawling right out of the ground!
He made birds, bulls, gnats,
Dogs, cats, snakes and bats.

When He put together the tree
He was quite sure
That this new creation
Would be part of His future.

Then He said, I really love these things I have made.
I've made moles to go down and birds to go up.
But I need something else.
So He shaped His hands, just like a cup.

He filled them with dirt
And shaped it like Him.
He gave it eyes
and hair—on a whim.

Hands, feet, mouth and ears,
Legs, tummy, arms and a nose.
A belly button!—Do you think he had a belly button?
Did he need one of those?

But man fell and began to sin.
God knew then (for His plans were good),
That the tree would have to be carved into wood.

HIS PLAN

God called the heavens into place
God spoke and shaped the human race
Blew spirit into dust of bone.

In love beyond all time and space
Creator met creation face to face
Together, they were not alone.

Light in shadowless starting days
Full communion in God's ways
The legacy of genesis was lost.

God restored His Paradigm
Returning to earth in the center of time
For a meeting at the cross.

He is the image of the invisible God, the firstborn
over all creation. For by Him all things were
created: things in heaven and on earth,
visible and invisible, whether thrones
or powers or rulers or authorities;
all things were created by Him
and for Him. He is before
all things, and in Him
all things hold
together.

Colossians 1:15-17

DIVINE LONGING

In the beginning, God spoke. He created the heavens, the earth, and everything in them by the word of His power. He fashioned man into His image and likeness from the dust of the earth, breathing His own life into the creature. Then He proclaimed that all the results were good; they had to be, because He spoke us into existence with words of holy love. When love is spoken, life and goodness spring forth.

God has so much love to give that He created sons and daughters just so He could lavish His affection upon us. Within each of us is the knowledge that we need His pure love to grow and to survive. We were made to receive the blessings of His words; we yearn for the tenderness of His touch. He is our Father, and we are His children. Absolutely nothing can replace the longing for His presence within our hearts.

When God blessed the original man with authority over the earth, He gave him permission to eat freely from every tree in the garden except one. God warned Adam that if he ate from the tree of the knowledge of good and evil, he would surely die. He clearly described the consequences to Adam and left the choice to him.

After Adam and Eve followed the serpent's suggestion and ate the forbidden fruit, their vision changed. At the exact moment that their eyes opened to the knowledge of good and evil, they experienced shame at their nakedness. God was still good, pure, and holy—but they were not. They could not see the truth about God, and they did not want to see the truth about themselves because their eyes were clouded. They withdrew from the intensity of His passion because His presence revealed the depths of their disobedience.

When God asked if they had eaten from the forbidden tree, Adam said, "She gave me of the tree, and I ate." Eve responded, "The serpent deceived me, and I ate" (Gen. 3:12-13 NKJV). They avoided taking responsibility; neither of them admitted their own guilt. Instead, they identified another as the evil doer and justified their own personal behavior. In Adam's eyes,

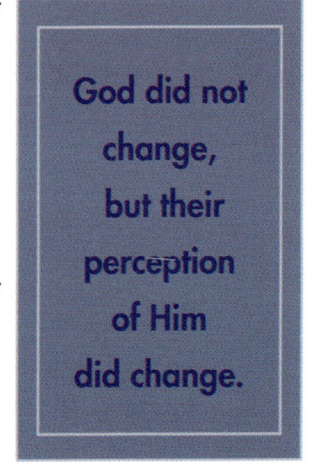

> **God did not change, but their perception of Him did change.**

compared to Eve—he was good. In Eve's eyes, compared to the serpent—she was also good. They were judging themselves by a new standard, a mixture of good and evil.

They were caught in a very painful situation. They still desired and required the Father's love, but for the first time, they felt unworthy to receive it. Since they refused to admit the truth about their own actions, they remained separated from the One whom they most needed. He had not changed, but their perceptions of Him had drastically changed. He continued to give His love, but they could not accept it.

Since we are Adam's descendants, we have inherited the same blurred vision and distorted view of truth. We compensate for the inability to receive His love by comparing ourselves with other humans. If we measure ourselves against people who are evil and do wicked deeds, we judge ourselves as good. When we pass our own tests of goodness, we conclude that we deserve to be loved, and we expect to receive that love from other people. However, no human love can satisfy the longing in our hearts for Him. By His original design, we require the nourishment of His presence and we thrive on the knowledge of His love for us. No acceptable substitute will satisfy our needs. Without Him, we build our lives upon the edge of a grand chasm of desire that can only be bridged by His heart.

The Bible chronicles God's attempts to reconcile with the sons and daughters of Adam and Eve. We see the Father pursuing man in constant faithfulness, but man responds in the faithlessness of sin. Many complained about the requirements of His holiness and turned away from His offers of love. It was easier for them to reject God's love and to pretend that they could find satisfaction from conditional human affections.

The human race needed someone to accept the guilt for our sin and yet fulfill the Father's demands for righteousness. Pure and sinless Jesus agreed to leave Heaven, become human, and take our place upon the cross. When God the Son stretched out His arms to die upon the cross, God the Father opened His arms to receive us back within His loving embrace. That is why "there is joy in the presence of God's angels when even one sinner repents" (Luke 15:10 NLT).

To help us understand the depth of the Father's joy when His children return to Him and choose to receive His love, Jesus told the following story:

A man had two sons. The younger son told his father, "I want my share of your estate now, instead of waiting until you die." So his father agreed to divide his wealth between his sons.

A few days later this younger son packed all his belongings and took a trip to a distant land, and there he wasted all his money on wild living. About the time his money ran out, a great famine swept over the land, and he began to starve. He persuaded a local farmer to hire him to feed his pigs. The boy became so hungry that even the pods he was feeding the pigs looked good to him. But no one gave him anything.

When he finally came to his senses, he said to himself, "At home even the hired men have food enough to spare, and here I am, dying of hunger! I will go home to my father and say, 'Father, I have sinned against both heaven and you, and I am no longer worthy of being called your son. Please take me on as a hired man.' " So he returned home to his father. And while he was still a long distance away, his father saw him coming. Filled with love and compassion, he ran to his son, embraced him and kissed him. His son said to him, "Father, I have sinned against both heaven and you, and I am no longer worthy of being called your son."

But his father said to the servants, "Quick! Bring the finest robe in the house and put it on him. Get a ring for his finger, and sandals for his feet. And kill the calf we have been fattening in the pen. We must celebrate with a feast. For this son of mine was dead and has now returned to life. He was lost, but now he is found." So the party began.

Luke 15:11-24 NLT

Every time that we come to our senses and admit we are sinners, we are restored to the Father's arms. Only His goodness will overcome our selfish natures, and when we accept His loving kindness, He celebrates! As we rest in His embrace, the overflow of His generous love overcomes the pain of separation, fulfilling the desires of our hearts.

Hear my prayer, O LORD;

let my cry for help come to you.

Do not hide your face from me

when I am in distress.

Turn your ear to me;

when I call, answer me quickly.

Psalm 102:1-2

THE ONLY HOPE I HAVE

PART 1

What is this craving of my soul? What is this need? What is this place of continual desire that never diminishes? Satisfaction only initiates a deeper hunger, pushing me to the very edge of restless pursuit. A pursuit towards fulfillment. A sharp demand to keep on seeking whatever will fit this hollow place in my heart. Forever inquiring of the Lord, "How long?" How long until every part is established in eternal contentment and rest? There is always another part left to cry out for a commission....a role....a duty....a chance to be and do something greater than the present insignificant existence.

> Where do I belong?....my soul cries out.
>   Why does this part of me feel this way?
>   What is it that I want so badly?
>   What do I want it for?
>   How can it be channeled into true usefulness?

If brought before You as a living sacrifice, can You set my spirit free? If laid on Your altar, will something valuable and pure ever come from this dirty mess? Can I have a purpose and a place in Your divine plan? Am I needed? Can this pot of messed-up clay actually be used to hold something of value? I don't even need to be made into beautiful clay, only useable clay. My soul requires Your attention and begs for recognition and purpose.

And one more problem—can I come just as I am?
I find myself powerless to be what I am not.
Can You take me just like this? Can I be acceptable to You?
Am I enough....even in this state of uselessness....with hard, unbroken clay?
There is nowhere else I can go, so here I am, just like this.
You are the only hope I have.

PART 2

The closer I get, the further I fall.
You have looked deep into my heart and stripped it bare.
Now all my thoughts and motives lay revealed before me.
How can I be so thoroughly human?
Could any heart be more deceitful and wicked?
You can read my thoughts. You can see my faithless heart.
You can see that all of the inclinations of my heart are impure and unwise. And You can see that my heart drags me where I do not want to go and holds me there by its wayward desire. You can see my chains. And yet, some small voice reminds me that You lead and guide me. Have I not said that I rely more on Your guidance than my ability to make a choice? Ever since I discovered the lying deceit of my heart, I have cried, "Lead me not into temptation!" because there is no doubt that I will fall. Just as Jesus cried the same words, He was aware that only grace could give Him the will to submission, obedience, and holiness
And the road my feet walk upon is called the road of mercy
    ····because I am at Your mercy.
Every time You leave me alone, I choose selfish weakness.
Only You can keep me from walking by my flesh. Alone, I will only bring about my own destruction. But You know how to keep me humble, dependent, broken, and terrified of my heart
    ····just let me see it for one day.
Only You can cause me to "go and sin no more."
Only You can break the chains.
Only You can allow me to escape the destruction prepared for me.
Only You can keep me from temptation.
Never forget that I am a wayward, ignorant, stupid child.
Save me, Father. I am the very worst.

*I am
pained
in
my very
heart.*

IN TIME

Hear feeble cries
Against God's times
By human minds;
Watch empires crash like toys,
Horns turn to tin,
Men revert to boys
Shaking sticks at the moon.

See angels come,
Sickles in hand
Answering prophetic prayer,
Trumpeting the time to men.
Abraham's children will turn again,
Dry bones begin to rattle and rise
Under the reddening moon.

> O my soul, my soul
> I am pained in my very heart!
> My heart makes a noise in me;
> I cannot hold my peace,
> Because you have heard, O my soul,
> The sound of the trumpet,
> The alarm of war.
>
> Jeremiah 4:19 NKJV

I'M NOT GOING TO CRY, I'M NOT GOING TO CRY!!!

I went to the grave today. This was to be strictly a "business" visit. I had ordered the marker for Bobby's grave within days after the funeral, but I had to go back and approve it once it came in. There has been no marker on his grave because of a lack of time to take care of it. When I got to the cemetery, I was informed that the marker had been already placed on the grave, at the request of another family member, and I would have to go out to the burial site to look at it.

Wow—I was completely unprepared for this one. As I drove onto the cemetery property before even knowing that I would have to *go out* to the grave, I felt myself saying, "I'm not going to cry, I'm not going to cry, I'm NOT going to cry!!" There I was, walking among the gravesites, searching for my husband's grave! I finally found the grave and the marker with Robert "Bobby" J. Apon. Yes, there it was in bronze—no doubt about it!

I had kept my children from the cemetery and the funeral home because I knew that I needed to make it clear to them where their Daddy was not. The younger children would have had a hard time separating everything in their hearts. It is interesting to look back and see how God had me preparing the children without realizing it. Last December, a young boy was murdered in our city. The news spread fast and the children were quite interested in the story. I felt prompted to take the older children to the funeral. I remember thinking, I can't believe I'm taking my children to a funeral without knowing the person or family. I also remember God telling me that they needed to experience a funeral without the emotions of knowing that person. Two years before that a very good friend of ours died soon after their grandfather died. Again, I felt the need for them to understand about the things related to funerals and death.

I set up an appointment at the funeral home and took them to meet with the director, to see around the place, and to have him answer their questions. Do you know that director was the same man who directed their Daddy's funeral? God does have ways of preparing us when we do not realize that we are being prepared.

I do plan to take my children to their Daddy's grave on Bobby's birthday, November 1st. I'm sure that they will want to take flowers and I'm sure we will reminisce about the special things they remember about their Daddy. I want them to always honor their Dad and this would be a good way to do that. Perhaps that is why there is a grave.

As I was driving home, thinking through everything, I could feel myself really wanting to cry—God whispered to my heart—it's okay if you cry. With that, deep in my spirit, I began to really cry. That's when it hurts—I'm not crying on the outside, but deep within, the tears are flooding my soul!

I saw a picture of a clay ball being beaten up by a potter. I told God that my heart is just constantly being beaten up—punched, twisted, mashed. It seems like our hearts are in a constant state of change unless we have allowed them to become hard. Then, the brokenness has to come in and the tears have to come to soften our hearts.

I was sharing that with my children during devotions tonight and Kayla finished the story. "I know, Mommy, what God is shaping that ball of clay into—a large cup so that He can pour His love, happiness and joy into it!" Wow, that's worth the shaping and the tears!

This afternoon Abigail wanted me to proofread a short essay she wrote for class tomorrow. I was not at all sure what I was going to read, but I took the paper and began to glance over it. Below is her essay. What a gift I was given today—money could never buy this.

My Favorite People and Why

by Abigail Apon

My first favorite person is Jesus. He became my Father about seven years ago and began to rule my life on May 17, 1999 when my Daddy died. He is my favorite person because He is one of the only people that I can look up to and call 'my Dad.' Well, He is the only one.

My second favorite is my Mom. It has been hard for her to be a widow and a mother of eight kids at one time. She keeps asking us, "Do you think we can do this, guys?" We all say, "Yes." She is my favorite person because I look up to her and her faith in God and us.

Troubled Waters

Threatened by despair, in days of pain, loss, emptiness and need,
    when we cannot solve our own problems or help ourselves,
        we look beyond ourselves—
            to someone or something 'other' to help us.

When we look to the cross we see
    Christ identified forever
        with every loss,
        with every need and pain,
        with every rejection, betrayal and grief.

    From the murderer's guilt to the infant's hungry cry,
    From holocausts to the hospitals' critical care units,
    HE took all the sin and suffering of mankind on Himself.
        Man's need for a god was met by God's love for man—
            At the cross.

PRODIGALS' PUZZLE

The container is broken, clearly abused
Moldy smells from stains of use
Foul reminders of mislaid youth
Mix with sighs and stifled cries.

Pieces were lost, children not born
Parts were broken, dreams were torn
Faded and frayed, all vision's unglued,
Hiding the hope of original hues.

The Father's pain for each lost child
Stirred the universe with love.
"What price will I pay
For all of the children
Who've strayed from My ways,
To restore the lost pieces
Wash out mold and stain
Refresh worn off colors
Remove ancient pain
To fulfill every promise
Call each home again?"

Some lost their way in the wilderness, in desert places;
they found no inhabited place.
Hungry and thirsty, their soul fainted.
In their peril they cried out to the Lord,
and He rescued them from their troubles.
He led them in a straight way to a settled place.

Psalm 107: 4-7 (adapted)

THE STAIRPORT

In the book, *The Heavens Opened*, the author described her experiences while on a visit to heaven. She was granted access to paradise by three sets of connected steps called a stairport. An angel directed her to run up the steps to escape an attack from the enemy. In his hands, the angel held a scarlet cord that was fastened to the bottom of the stairs, and as she progressed up the staircase, the angel pulled up the first section behind her by tugging on the cord. Eventually, she finished climbing up, and the remaining two sections were also pulled up behind her. The angel said that she was "safe after climbing the second set of stairs, but to be really safe, [she] needed to pass the third [set]."[1] When they reached the top of the staircase, they were in heaven.

The author's husband described the meaning of the stairport in the following manner:

> The scarlet cord that is secured to the first section of the stairway into heaven represents the first stage of redemption through the Cross of Calvary (Josh. 2:18). This is the shed blood of Christ that releases us from guilt and separation from God that was caused by our sins (Rev. 1:5). The way is now open to the throne of God by faith (Heb. 10:22) through hope (Heb. 7:19) in the Lord Jesus.
>
> The second section of the stairway is the second stage of redemption through the cross of Calvary. It is the release from the power of sin by the death of the totally corrupt corporate spiritual heart of the human race. This happened when the old human race died with Christ on Calvary. God gives those who would believe in His Son a new heart that lives by the resurrection life of the Lord (Eph. 2:10; Rom. 6:6-8; 2 Cor. 5:14-17; Col. 3:3; Gal. 2:20).
>
> The third section secures one's position in the heavenly realm with Christ 'far above all rule and authority and power and dominion' of the enemy (Eph. 1:21). It is to live in God (Col. 3:3) the heavenly life of love, ministering to His needs (Ps. 65:4; Rev. 3:12). It is the place of the disciple who continually bears about in his body the sentence of death from the same, inner cross to his own self-expression that Jesus bore daily here on the earth (2 Cor. 4:10; 2 Cor. 1:9; Matt. 16:24; Phil. 2:7). It is the final stage of overcoming the enemies of God, where the soul life (mind, emotions and will) of Christ Jesus is being imparted to the believer (Matt. 16:25). It is the place of

---

1. Anna Rountree, *The Heavens Opened* (Creation House: Lake Mary, Florida. 1999). p. 3. Used by permission of the author.

the overcoming Christian in every generation (Rev. 2:7, 11, 17, 26-28; 3:5, 12, 21). The disciple who overcomes the world, the flesh, and the devil as the Lord Jesus overcame them seeks only the Living God, in comparison with whom all things are as rubbish (Rev. 3:21; Col. 3:1; Phil. 3:8).[1]

After reading about the stairport, I marveled at this simple yet profound picture of the gospel. There is no other way to live in God's presence except by a journey that begins at the cross. The pressures and battles of this earthly life drive us to a place where we have to admit how helpless and hopeless we are apart from Him. You and I need His strength, His love and affection, His holiness and His peace. We desperately need Him and His completed work at the cross for access to a life that is not of this world.

If we merely *observe* what Jesus did for us, we are still separated from Him. Instead, He invites us to walk with Him in the way of the cross. By the power of the Holy Spirit, we can take up the cross and travel with Him every step of the way. At the end of our upward climb, we will be like Him, and He will present us to His beloved Father. We choose to begin that awesome journey whenever we embrace Him on the cross.

---

1. Ibid., 118.

2 Love's Answer is Redemption

> The Lord will fulfill His purpose for me;
> Your love, O LORD, endures forever—
> Do not abandon the works of Your hands.
>
> Psalm 138:8

But God demonstrates his own love for us in this: While we were still sinners, Christ died for us.

Since we have now been justified by his blood, how much more shall we be saved from God's wrath through him!

For if, when we were God's enemies, we were reconciled to him through the death of his Son, how much more, having been reconciled, shall we be saved through his life!

Not only is this so, but we also rejoice in God through our Lord Jesus Christ, through whom we have now received reconciliation.

Romans 5:8–11

THE CRUCIFIXION

His Father called Him, "My Beloved Son." He returned His Father's love and He sought His Father's glory, not His own. He fulfilled the laws of His Father's Kingdom and lived by His Father's ways. Although He was Creator of the Universe and a King above all Kings, His kingdom was not of this world. Fully God, He was also fully man.

He was sensitive and strong, gentle and lowly, with absolute authority over man, nature, and the supernatural realm. His mind was unquestionably brilliant; He confounded every scholar who questioned Him. His emotions were pure. He took advantage of none. He was motivated by compassionate love. His love for His Father was unbounded and ruled His life. He did only what He saw His Father doing. His compassion for man broke all human limits for giving. He fed the hungry, healed the sick, restored sanity to the demonized, gave hope and purpose to the lost and broken, brought the dead back to life, remained loyal to faithless friends, and forgave sinners. He kept ALL His Father's rules and became humility, mercy, meekness, joy, peace, truth, faith, hope and love. He did nothing wrong. Men accused Him falsely. The crowd cried, "Crucify Him!"

Religious men rejected His kingdom for Caesar's. Soldiers dressed Him up in royal robes like a king of this world and mocked Him. They spat upon Him and their spit stuck to Him. A crown of thorns was set upon His head, scratching and jabbing His scalp with pain. Men hit His head till it was tender with welts. Hardened men struck Him with their hands, stinging and bruising His body. They lashed Him, slashing and digging down to the bone, gouging hunks of flesh from His back with leather thongs laced with metal or bone. When He was weakened, wounded, and weary from watching without sleep, a heavy wooden cross was put upon His shoulders and He was commanded to carry it to Golgotha, the place of the skull. He stumbled and fell. Another was called to carry the cross, but no one reached out a hand to give Him help. His clothes were stripped; He watched men gamble to get them. Men tried to drug Him to dull the pain and dim His mind, but He refused. His lacerated back was pressed into the hard wood of the cross. Blood ran. His body was stretched, without support. Nails driven through His flesh held Him fast. The agony went through Him. Strangers stared at Him. Death by excruciating suffocation began. He bore insults and jeers. They dared Him to prove that He was God. The chief priests, religious men, reproached Him. They were derisive and mocked Him with scorn. His mother and His closest friend watched His humiliation. His Father turned His back on Him. He thirsted. When every prophesy of scripture had been fulfilled, He cried out with a loud voice, "It is finished" and He died. In death, He entrusted His Spirit into His Father's hands. By trusting His Spirit to His Father, even while burdened with our sin, He made a statement of belief in the Father's goodness. The separation could not be permanent because of their history of perfect love. In the most horrible form of capital punishment under Roman law, men of our race killed their own Creator. We killed Him. No evil thought of retaliation or accusation came to His mind or entered His soul. He forgave. He trusted. He loved.

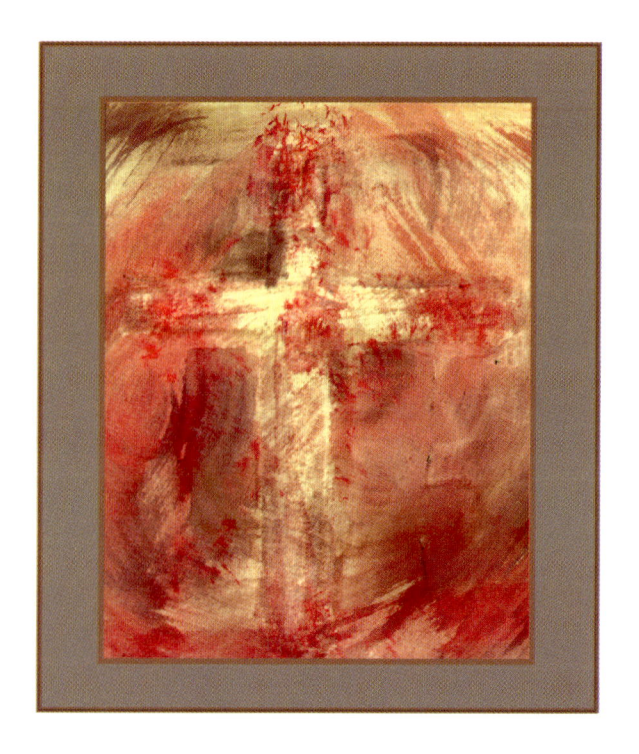

Surely he took up our infirmities and carried our sorrows,
yet we considered him stricken by God, smitten by him and afflicted.
But he was pierced for our transgressions,
he was crushed for our iniquities;
the punishment that brought us peace was upon him,
and by his wounds we are healed.
We all, like sheep, have gone astray,
each of us has turned to his own way;
and the LORD has laid on him the iniquity of us all.
He was oppressed and afflicted,
yet he did not open his mouth;
he was led like a lamb to the slaughter,
and as a sheep before her shearers is silent,
so he did not open his mouth.

Isaiah 53:4-7

THAT DAY

What did men say that day, that day?
That Day, what words did He hear?

What were the sounds on Calvary's hill?
Did mocking words from Caesar's men,
      A cadre commissioned to kill,
      Cut the air with echoing chill?

What were the sounds on Calvary's hill?
Did all talk stop
      While pounding hammers beat
      Bitter nails into hands and feet?

What were the sounds on Calvary's hill?
As priests and elders sneered
      And twisted the wind with ugly jeers—
      Did the faithful bow their ears in fear?

What were the sounds on Calvary's hill?
Did the women who followed,
      Keeping watch from afar,
      Soften the air with weeping?

What were the sounds on Calvary's hill?
What about John, His beloved friend,
      Did John watch Him die
      In silence, stifling moans and groaning cries?

What were the sounds on Calvary's hill?
Was His mother still,
      Feeling the sword pierce her soul
      As she yielded again to words foretold?

What were the sounds on Calvary's hill?
Were angelic hosts stilled in awe
      At fulfillment of the ancient law
      And the mystery of God's will?

What were the sounds on Calvary's hill
When victory was won,
      As darkness hid the sun,
      And Satan was defeated
      With His cry that "It is done!"?

One centurion cried, "This innocent man,
Was surely the Son of God!"

Mark 15:39 and Luke 23:47 (adapted)

HIS OBEDIENCE: John 19: 28-30

N. J. Suire

Thoughts and reflections on one aspect of Jesus' death.

The Scriptural theme of rebels against God who can become right with Him by trusting in the finished work of Jesus' death on the cross is a glorious truth. However, too much of an emphasis on our personal justification before God can sometimes mask the fact that God is still a Holy God, One Who is still interested in justice and righteousness. We sometimes divorce the God of justice from the God Who justifies sinners on the basis of trust in Christ.

Jesus' death accomplished two things. First, His death actually paid the fines sinful man received by breaking God's law. For example, suppose a person breaks into another's house, steals various household items, and is later apprehended. A judge can impose penal sanctions, fines, or jail time on the thief. Jesus' death paid for our penal sanctions, our eternal punishment, death, and estrangement from God. In death, He received the sanctions required against us for breaking God's Holy Law so that our negative actions will not be held against us. Theologians call this aspect of Jesus' death His passive obedience; *He* died and passively received all of the wrath of the Father that was meant for sinful man.

Second, and just as important, Jesus' perfect life of obedience to the Father, which culminated in His work on the cross, met the positive demands that God made in His law, but were impossible for us to fulfill. For example, imagine how difficult it is for us to drive an automobile within the legal speed limit law one hundred percent of the time. Jesus, in a sense, drove the speed limit for us so that we look as if we have never driven too fast. Theologians call this aspect of Jesus' death His active obedience; *His* perfect keeping of all the moral code of God somehow can be transferred to our account. The Ten Commandments have both a positive and a negative thrust. Although stated in the negative, each commandment was meant by God to have a positive outward thrust in our lives. For example, the Ninth commandment states, "Don't lie." Jesus' passive death on the cross paid our penalty whenever we do lie. However, the flip side to the ninth commandment is, "Tell the truth." Again, Jesus' active obedience to the Father in always telling the truth was also given to us in the great transaction of justification by faith. Regarding the law, we are covered, positively and negatively, by Jesus' death. Therefore, we do not need to live a life of shame. Romans 5:19 says, "For just as through the disobedience of the one man (Adam) the many were made sinners, so also through the obedience of the one man (Jesus) the many will be made righteous."

The entire Gospel of John is concerned with the theme of Jesus' obedience to the Father: "My Father is always at His work to this very day, and I, too, am working" (John 5:17) and "I have brought You glory on earth by completing the work You gave me to do" (John 17:4). In John 19:28-30, John highlights the theme of Jesus as the obedient servant of God by giving a small glimpse into one minute area of Jesus' life. Remember, God is in the details.

In verse 28, the scene is one of intense suffering and thirst in the hot Middle Eastern sun. Jesus is about to die. He maintained His composure and persevered in obeying the Father in the details of His suffering moments before His death. Jesus knew He had to request a drink on the cross to fulfill Psalm 69:21, "They gave me vinegar for my thirst." John wants his readers to understand that every part of Jesus' passion was not only in the Father's plan of redemption but a consequence of the Son's direct obedience to it. John, therefore, wrote, "Jesus, knowing that all things had already been accomplished, in order that the Scripture might be fulfilled, said, 'I am thirsty.' A jar full of sour wine was standing there; so they put a sponge full of the sour wine upon a branch of hyssop, and brought it up to His mouth.

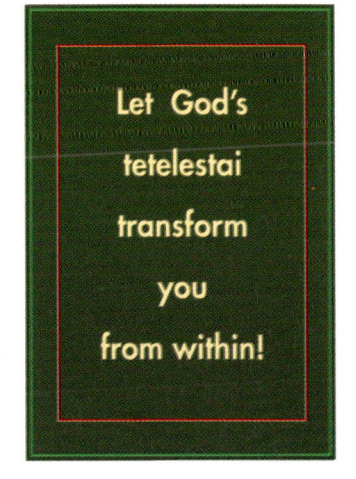

Let God's tetelestai transform you from within!

When Jesus therefore had received the sour wine, He said, 'It is finished!' And he bowed His head, and gave up His spirit" (John 19:28-30 NASB).

"It is finished," *Tetelestai!* in the Greek, was probably the loud cry of Mark 15:37, "And Jesus uttered a loud cry, and breathed His last" (NASB). *Tetelestai* means a transaction completed. The term is still used in Greece as a business stamp. Jesus *knew* that his work of obedience to the Father was finished, completed, done to the fullest extent.

Nothing further needs to be done. There is no need to impress God by our obedience. Jesus did it all by His obedience. No one would take a piece of sandpaper to a perfectly finished table, hand-waxed many times by an expert craftsman, in an attempt to improve on it!

How we need to hear the word *tetelestai* ring in our hearts and minds always. Motivated by guilt? Many are. It is surprising how many of our actions are motivated by guilt. Haunted by shame from your past? Fearful of the Day of Judgment? Let God's *tetelestai* transform you from within!   **TETELESTAI !**

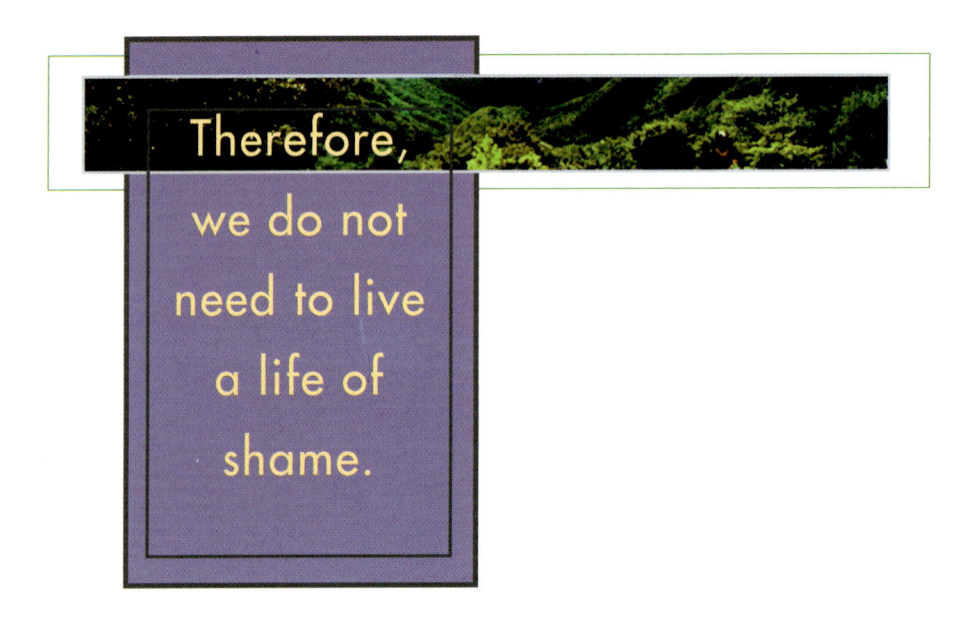

> Therefore, we do not need to live a life of shame.

OUR PRAYER

Father, forgive us
    for we have despised
        and trivialized the cross.

Father, forgive us
    for the times we make ourselves comfortable in a culture
        that wears crosses to match our costumes.

Father, forgive us
    for avoiding the reality of the Lamb who has been slain
        and is worthy to open the scrolls of heaven.

Father, forgive us
    for we have not seen Jesus.

> OUR FATHER WILL FORGIVE US!

JESUS: THE CHRIST

Flesh?
Yes. Songs and sores,
"Oh sacred heart now bleeding"
All man-defined was there.

Spirit?
You bet.
Angels sang. Demons trembled.
God Himself
Made blood sacrifice
In birth and death
For you.

This is how God showed his love among us:
He sent his one and only Son into the world
that we might live through him.

1 John 4:9

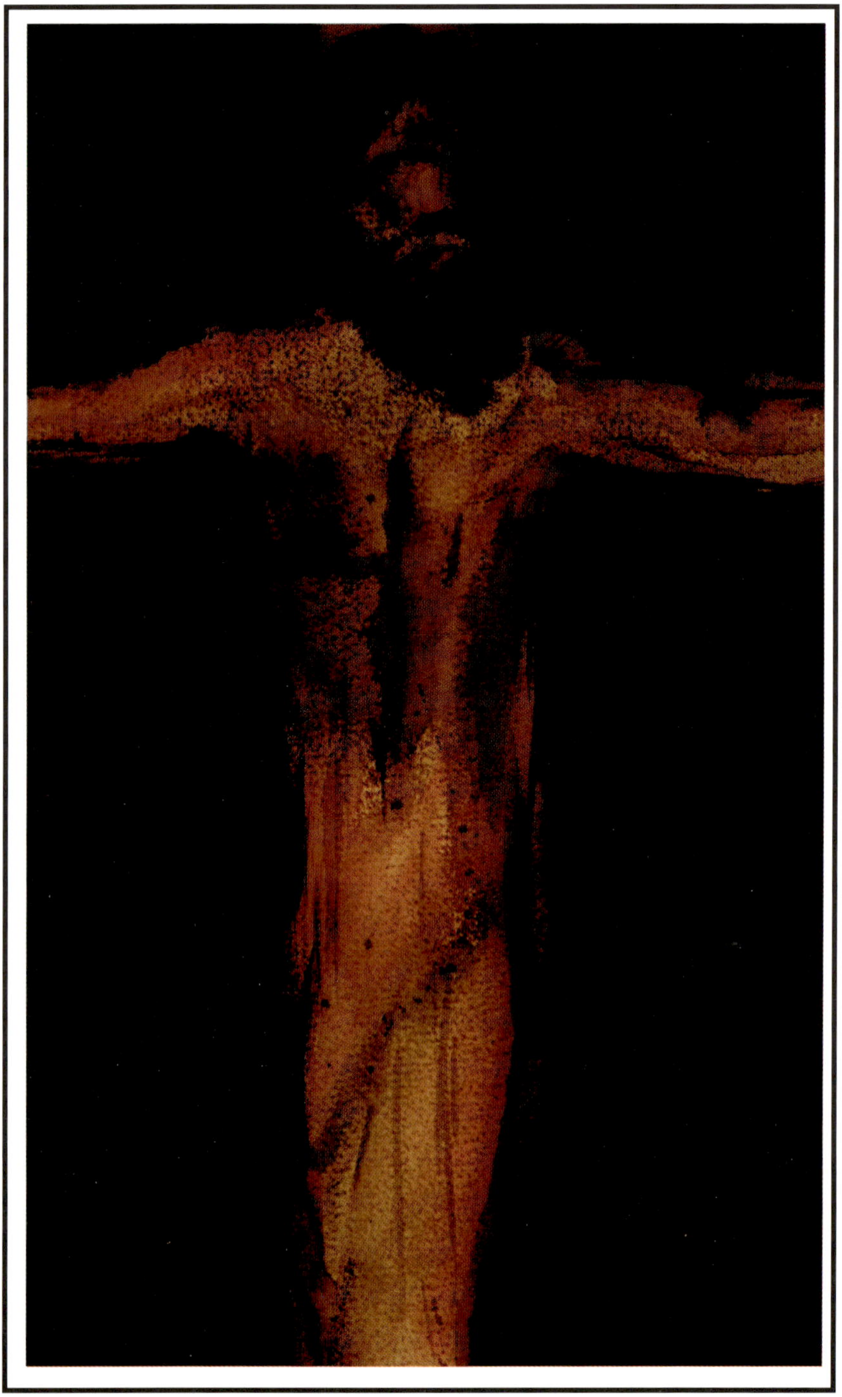

"MY GOD, MY GOD, WHY HAVE YOU FORSAKEN ME?"

Ross Nelson, founding pastor, Vineyard Christian Fellowship, Elgin, Illinois

For me, the most impacting words spoken by our Lord Jesus Christ from the cross are these: "My God, my God, why have you forsaken me?" (Mark 15:34). The thought that our loving heavenly Father, living in a holy and perfectly united relationship with His dear Son, was separated from His suffering Son—abandoning Him, turning from His presence, and leaving Him helpless upon the cross—awes me. To my finite mind, it is incomprehensible that God could do this, let alone allow it to happen. Nevertheless, Jesus Himself, in taking our sin on the cross, experienced the agony of His own Father's rejection.

It has been said that hell could be described as the total absence of the presence of God. When Jesus cried out, "My God, my God, why have you forsaken me?"—He encountered that definition of hell. Now the indelible mark which the Holy Spirit has placed upon my heart is that Jesus, my Lord, has removed from me forever the deserved prospect of eternal banishment. Can a greater portrait of love be seen than in our Lord's utter forsakenness?

PUTTING ALL OUR EXPECTANCIES IN THE BLOOD OF THE CROSS

C. S. Kellough (Used with permission.)

The following truths were taken from the outline of a powerful talk on the cross. They have been used as a prayer model by a few believers and the fruit is still unfolding: lives have been changed, broken relationships restored, and family members have come to faith in Christ.

I.

1. My self centeredness, my corrupt, rebel nature, my old man was put to death—that the God centered nature of Jesus, the new man might come alive in me.
2. Jesus was punished for my guilt— that I might be forgiven and have peace.
3. Jesus was wounded—that I might be healed.
4. Jesus was made sin—that I might be righteous.
5. Jesus died my death—that I might share His life.
6. Jesus was made a curse— that I might be freed from curses and receive blessings.
7. Jesus endured my poverty—that I might share in the riches of His kingdom.
8. Jesus bore my shame—that I might share His glory.
9. Jesus endured my rejection— that I might have His acceptance with the Father.
10. Jesus was cut off—that I might be joined to God eternally.
11. Jesus disarmed the rulers and authorities and triumphed over them— that in Him I may overcome and find victory.
12. Jesus experienced my darkness—that I might have light in my heart to give the light of the knowledge of God.
13. Jesus took my offense—that I might be free.
14. Jesus' cross enables me to be crucified to the world and the world crucified to me.
15. Christ, the crucified, is the power of God and the wisdom of God.

II.

As we put our expectancies in the pure,
    perfect, sinless blood of Jesus,
    the power that was released at the cross
    flows into our own souls and changes us.

As Jesus took all the evil that was due to our rebellion upon Himself,
    all of the good due to His sinless obedience became available to us.

The work that He finished at the Cross
    becomes an ongoing process in our lives as we take the cross,
    and in faith we appropriate all He did for us.

    The blood of Jesus redeems us.[1]
    The blood of Jesus pleads for us at the Mercy Seat of God.[2]
    The blood of Jesus makes atonement for us; it covers our sins.[3]
    The blood of Jesus cleanses us from sin.[4]
    The blood of Jesus declares us righteous.[5]
    The blood of Jesus quickens us and gives us new life.[6]
    The blood of Jesus cuts covenant for us
        and brings us into covenant relationship with the Father.[7]
    The blood of Jesus consecrates us; it sets us apart,
        separates us from the world, the flesh, and the devil,
        and brings us into the Kingdom of God.[8]

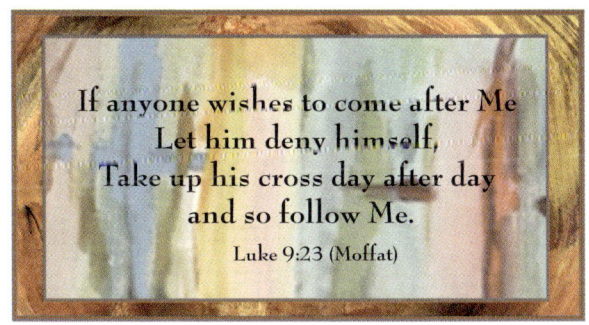

> If anyone wishes to come after Me
> Let him deny himself,
> Take up his cross day after day
> and so follow Me.
> Luke 9:23 (Moffat)

[1](Ephesians 1:7)   [2](Lev. 16:15; Heb. 9:12)   [3](Romans 3:25)   [4](1John 1:7)
[5](Romans 5:9)   [6](Lev. 17:11; John 6:54)   [7](Hebrews 9:15; 13:20)   [8](1 Cor. 6:19-20)

THIS PAIN

Christ's humanity, condensed—
"My Father, if it is possible, may this cup be taken from me."
This prayer, I know.
Not this. Not now.
Spare me this pain.
Desire exposed to the One who can fulfill.
Desire's choice—to demand or to submit.
May my choice be Christ's.
"Yet not as I will, but as You will."

He said to them,
"Pray that you may not have to face temptation!"
Then he went off by himself, about a stone's throw away,
and falling on his knees, prayed in these words
"Father, if you are willing, take this cup away from me—
but it is not my will, but yours, that must be done."
And an angel from heaven appeared, strengthening him.

Luke 22:40-43 Phillips

ALONE

My cup was empty.
All hope was gone.
I was alone.

Your cup was empty.
Your Father was gone.
You hung alone.

I feared Your faith might be a lie.
I sought Your cross
Through hard and hurting eyes.

I couldn't look away.
I cried through unbelief
And tried to pray.

God warmed the coldness of my heart
Faith slowly opened up in me
A growing Love, Alive and Free.

Hope bursting, I began to sing.
Trust woke to find beginning wings
Rising up from Heavenly Springs.

THE TREE THAT WOULD NOT DIE

A tree called Love

Made in Love

Shaped in Love

Grew in Love

Rooted and grounded in Love

That Family Tree

That Tree of Life

For God so loved the world that he gave his only Son,
so that everyone who believes in him will not perish but have eternal life.

John 3:16 NLT

THE BLOOD THAT COVERS ME : A Song

Broken and bleeding I see Him
Blood flowing down from the tree
And as I look in His eyes, He's looking back at me.
I bow my head in sorrow.
I dare not gaze upon His face
For I've abused His mercies, and trampled on His grace.
    But He takes me in His arms, and causes me to see,
    That He gladly shed His Blood, and poured it over me.

Chorus: I've been immersed in the Blood, the Blood that covers me.
          I'm sanctified in Him, His mercies never cease
          I'm crucified in Christ, and I no longer live
          For Jesus lives in me. And in His brokenness I see
          the Blood that covers me.

This journey through life is a battle
At war with forces unseen
And in my strength I find, it leaves my life unclean.
So I make my way to the River
To wash this guilt from my eyes.
The face I see in the water, I do not recognize.
    But He gently lifts my head, and once again I see,
    that He daily takes His blood, and pours it over me.

Repeat Chorus followed by *Interlude:*

It covers me—it covers me—your blood it covers me—and now I see—

I've been immersed
in YOUR Blood,
The Blood that covers me.
I'm sanctified in YOU,
YOUR mercies never cease.
I'm crucified in Christ,
And I no longer live
'CAUSE LORD YOU live in me.
And in YOUR brokenness I see
the blood that covers me.

© Mighty Warrior Music INTL. Used by permission.

GETHSEMANE

Gethsemane's for tourists now.
The gnarled trees,
Their memories trapped
In sap long dried,
Belie the triumphant fact
That You're alive!

It was a horrible night.
Halloween, late night spook shows,
Pogroms, massacres,
and Satan's dark secrets
From the source of time,
Burst with a blackness
Of hate over Your hallowed head.
But You held on,
Held on in hope, faith,
And love that looked beyond,
And turned the desecration of Your body
on the cross into Holy Sacrifice.

Give Gethsemane's strength to me.
The gnarled trees,
Their memories trapped
In sap long dried,
Testify that death has died!

Garden of Gethsemane Jerusalem, 1993

Yellow stars which Jewish citizens of Germany, Poland, and occupied countries of Europe were forced to wear during the Nazi regime.

THE CROSS

The cross
    doorway to Life.

Death's defeat
    and entrance to Love.

The place of Union
    and deep communion.

His life providing
    In Him abiding.

His place of rest,
    It is my fervent quest.

Come dine with the thief
    on Broken Bread
    and Poured out Wine.

THE WEAPON OF CHOICE

On the Cross, Jesus voluntarily separated Himself from the love of His Father so that our fellowship with Him could be restored. Only Heaven can reveal what His Father must have endured as He watched the sufferings of His beloved Son. It may be that the intensity of their pain caused the violent earthquake which followed His death. Graves opened and rocks split apart (Matt. 27:51-2).

Jesus chose to restrain the power of the universe within His being so that He could die in our place. When He rose victoriously three days later, His power was unleashed from captivity. The force of His release from death's grip also raised to life other dead bodies of godly men and women. They came out of their opened tombs and appeared to many in Jerusalem (v. 53). When the payment for our sin had been paid, the power over the grave was broken once and for all.

Jesus conquered the devil's power over death, hell, and the grave by dying. Today, the cross is still a weapon. It defeats our enemies every time, but we must choose to pick it up and use it. In His hands, the cross became a sword that shattered man's definition of peace. In fact, using the sword is still a declaration of war; it comes to set a man against his father and a daughter against her mother (Matt.10:34–5). The cross is the actual instrument upon which Jesus chose to die, but it is also a powerful symbol of what the place of the cross should represent to us. To form a cross, we need two pieces: one of them is arranged vertically and the other one lies horizontally. When placed upon each other physically, there is a place of meeting. Every time that we come to that juncture in our journey with the Lord, we have a choice to make: will we continue walking in the ways of man or change directions and move up into the ways of His heart?

Every time that we pray, "Your kingdom come. Your will be done, on earth as it is in heaven," we have just asked the Lord to bring a crossroads into the situation. In fact, Jesus spoke the exact words of the intersection when He cried out to His Father, "Not my will (horizontal), but thine be done" (vertical).

We need to remember that the devils are already intimately acquainted with the power of the cross because they were completely defeated at Calvary. Is it any wonder that our enemies oppose us every time that we are given an opportunity to choose the cross for ourselves? Not a single thought, word, or deed from hell is able to stand before the power of the cross, for every time that we choose His will over our own will, His life is birthed from our death. If the captain of our force is Jesus, and we are to follow in His footsteps, we too must learn to wield the sword that is shaped like a cross.

As we look to the cross, and cry out, "Lord, I want to see!"

    He opens our eyes, and we see that
    He has borne *our* griefs,
    He has carried *our* sorrows,
    He was pierced for *our* transgressions,
    He was bruised for *our* iniquities,
    And the chastisement of *our* peace was upon Him.
                Isaiah 53: 4-5
               (*Adapted from Rotherham*)

JESUS KEEP ME NEAR THE CROSS

I want to believe that love never fails.
But if LOVE never fails, then what failed? Did God fail? Did I fail?
If I failed, why didn't God stop me from failing?
I'm sorry. I know that all this doubt does not sound like me,
but I am in so much pain.
I can't even find Jesus here, even though He is my most frequently
discussed subject. And as tears run down my face, I am asking God
some really hard questions. Where is He? Where was He?
When we have needed Him so desperately, why didn't He come?
Before weeks of pain turned into months of pain which became years of pain.
Where was my Healer that we discussed every day?
Pain has so clouded my view that it is hard for me to picture the cross····
Oh, there it is. There's the cross. I can see Him now····He's bleeding.
The blood is red····crimson red. Oh, and now, there is His face.
He is crying. Now He is screaming, "Why have you forsaken ME!"
So that is where He was all these years: on His cross.
He has been trying to pay for all this sorrow, sickness, grief, and sin, but
no one seemed to let Him. Oh, I see the people now. They are walking
by····walking right by the cross without looking at it. Oh, why won't they
look up? If they would, they would see the blood, they would see His
tears····but no, they are looking down····what are they looking at?
Oh, it's themselves.
Wow. It is not that loved failed. It is not that God (who is Love) failed.
It is not even that we failed. It is that we were UNWILLING TO FAIL.
If only we were willing to admit our failures, we could learn how to
place those failures on the cross····because Jesus paid for all of them!
Now I know! We can be free! We get to be failures!
Because He is perfect, we can exchange all that we are for all that He is
because of the cross!!! Oh, praise the Lord! It is OK if I fail, because He
cannot fail and Love cannot fail. Therefore I cannot fail as long as I place
all my failures on the cross and walk in the willingness/freedom to fail!
I don't have to fear failure anymore. His perfect love casts out all my fear.
Nothing can save me except His blood and His cross
and that's OK because that's enough.
Jesus, don't let me pass by the cross and miss the whole reason for it:
to TAKE my sin. I don't have to keep it.

adapted from **THE IMITATION OF CHRIST**

Thomas à Kempis, 1380-1471

Why do you fear to take up the Cross which leads you to a kingdom? In the Cross is salvation, in the Cross is life, in the Cross is protection against our enemies, in the Cross is infusion of heavenly sweetness, in the Cross is strength of mind, in the Cross there is joy of spirit, the height of virtue and the perfection of holiness. There is no salvation of the soul, nor hope of everlasting life but in the Cross. Take up therefore your Cross and follow Jesus,[1] and you shall go into life everlasting. He went before, bearing His Cross,[2] and died for you on the Cross that you also may bear your Cross and desire to die on the Cross. For if you be dead with Him, you shall also in like manner live with Him.[3] And if you share His punishment, you shall also share His glory.[4]

Behold! In the Cross all does consist, and in our dying upon the cross all lies; for there is no other way to life and true inward peace, but the way of the holy Cross, and of daily dying to the life of self. Walk where you will, seek what you will, you shall not find a higher way above, or a safer way below, than the way of the holy Cross. . . .

The Cross is always ready, and waits for you everywhere. You cannot escape it wherever you run; for wherever you go, you carry yourself with you, and shall always find yourself. Turn above, turn below, turn without, turn within, and in all these places you shall find the Cross; and everywhere of necessity you must hold your patience, if you will have inward peace, and win an everlasting crown. For if you bear the Cross cheerfully, it will bear you, and lead you to the desired end.

From Thomas à Kempis, *Imitation of Christ* (Grosset & Dunlap, 1976), The Second Book, Chapter XII, Of the Kings high way of the holy Cross, 92-93.

[1] Luke 14:27   [2] John 19:17   [3] Gal. 2:20; Rom. 6:8   [4] 2 Cor. 1:5

LITANY OF THE MOST PRECIOUS BLOOD

Lord have mercy.
Christ have mercy.
Lord have mercy.
Christ hear us.
Christ graciously hear us.
God our Father in heaven, have mercy on us.
God the Son, Redeemer of the world, have mercy on us.
God the Holy Ghost have mercy on us.
Holy Trinity one God, have mercy on us.
Blood of Christ,
the only begotten Son of the Eternal Father save us.
Blood of Christ, the Word of God made flesh
Blood of Christ of the new and eternal covenant
Blood of Christ, in His agony running down to the ground
Blood of Christ welling up under the scouring
Blood of Christ flowing beneath the crown of thorns
Blood of Christ poured out upon the cross
Blood of Christ which paid for our salvation
Blood of Christ which purchased our forgiveness
Blood of Christ to nourish and cleanse our souls
Blood of Christ, torrent of mercy
Blood of Christ overcoming all powers of darkness
Blood of Christ strengthening martyrs
Blood of Christ giving courage in danger
Blood of Christ giving confessors' endurance
Blood of Christ source of virginity
Blood of Christ helping the burdened
Blood of Christ comforting in sorrow
Blood of Christ giving hope to the repentant
Blood of Christ consoling the dying
Blood of Christ refreshing hearts with peace
Blood of Christ assuring us of everlasting life
Blood of Christ opening wide the gates of heaven
Blood of Christ worthy of all praise and glory
Lamb of God,
who takes away the sins of the world,
Have mercy on us.

Text: 13th century, adapted from the Basilica of the Holy Blood in Brugge, Flanders
Design: Rosie Curtiss

CHOICES

        I see two cups—
       One's crystal clear
        The wine within
            Is light,
     Tinged with a blush
       Of amber gold
Sparkling with bubbles
           of life.

I can't see through
The other cup—
The wine is dark within
Shaded with hues
Of crimson red
Thick and heavy
With sin.

LEGALISM, LICENSE AND LOVE

Recently, my heart was broken by an e-mail from a tormented Christian who came to faith in Jesus from a lifestyle style of sexual sin. The Christians around this young person "handcuffed" sinners, demanding behavior modification and change through law. It didn't work. The person struggled, floundered, and finally gave up, saying, "I'm exasperated with these Christians. I need to be loved and cared for. I've found a Bible study where they don't think my sin is wrong. They don't think the Bible is the Bible, but I get acceptance and grace there."

A human heart—hungry for love—was caught between legalism saying "Shape up" and license saying "Do what you please." and thus, didn't hear the truth. Between those streams stands the cross that the Son of God died upon. At that cross sinners (and *all* have sinned) can find forgiveness, receive the Father's love, and find victory over sin.

Truth is easily lost when we lose sight of the cross. The legalist replaces God's grace and the power of the cross with personal effort and works of law. Legalism is man centered; the cross is Christ centered. The legally driven system is selfish and ungrateful. At the cross, the potential for gratefulness and worship is limitless because the love given to you is limitless. In the legal system there is no joy. In the cross, the potential for joy is unending. The legal system has no intimacy or mercy, for it subconsciously chooses to perform for the Father, rather than to live out of a tender, honest, and mutually loving relationship. In the love of the cross, the potential for intimacy is unlimited.

The law is the schoolmaster leading us to Christ. Imagine sitting in a classroom where the teacher says, "Don't commit adultery." We think we can follow that commandment until we hear the next lesson, "If you look at a woman with lust in your heart, you've already committed adultery." Our honest response should be, "Whoa—I'm in trouble. I'm a sinner." Then Christ reveals the cross. He says, "I will take your sin upon myself. Identify with Me in My death and I will give you My

Resurrection Life." At that point, some get up from their desks, run to the teacher and say, "You know what, I think I can do what you are describing. I think if I wear blinders twenty-four hours a day, I will not lust in my heart."

The legalist tries to fulfill God's law in his own power. At its core is a confidence in his own ability to do right, be good, and win God's approval. Legalism is not the pursuit, even passionately, of any given law, but trusting in the law for what only the gospel can do. Legalism says, "The law is doable. Just do it, you will be righteous." Since our flesh is desperately proud, independent, and self-righteous we are drawn to legalism as instinctively as iron filings to a magnet. Apart from the work of the Spirit, we will surely drift into its chains.

License also arises from misunderstanding the law and the gospel. At its core is a flippancy, an apathy, and a disdain for the law. The license student sits in class, hears the law, sees the cross, and then gets up and tells the teacher, "What you're teaching me is a bunch of rubbish. It's ridiculous. It doesn't apply to me. It has no relevance in my life. I'm out of here." Ironically, license shares the same sources as legalism. It is similarly proud, self-righteous, and independent, but expresses it by rejecting God's law and resting in autonomous self-law.

License misunderstands the law by trivializing the true standards of a holy God who offers us an opportunity to identify with Christ in His death, burial, and resurrection. It misunderstands the gospel by trivializing its intention to radically transform us. The truth of the love for His Father that led Jesus to the cross and the truth of the Father's love for His Son on the cross is powerful enough to change our attitude toward God, and it is powerful enough to change us from the inside out. The truth of the love on the cross challenges us to skirt the pitfalls of license and legalism and to seek God's power, asking Him to give us mercy and grace for the obedience of faith.

WASHED CLEAN

Born of His Spirit
      united as one,
Filthy with sin
      washed with His Son.

Cleansed of all wrong
      we fly as a dove
In perfect delight
      with whispers of love.

Abigail Apon, age 10

For by a single offering He has forever completely
cleansed and perfected those who are consecrated and made holy.

Hebrews 10:14 AMP

Yesterday the War began

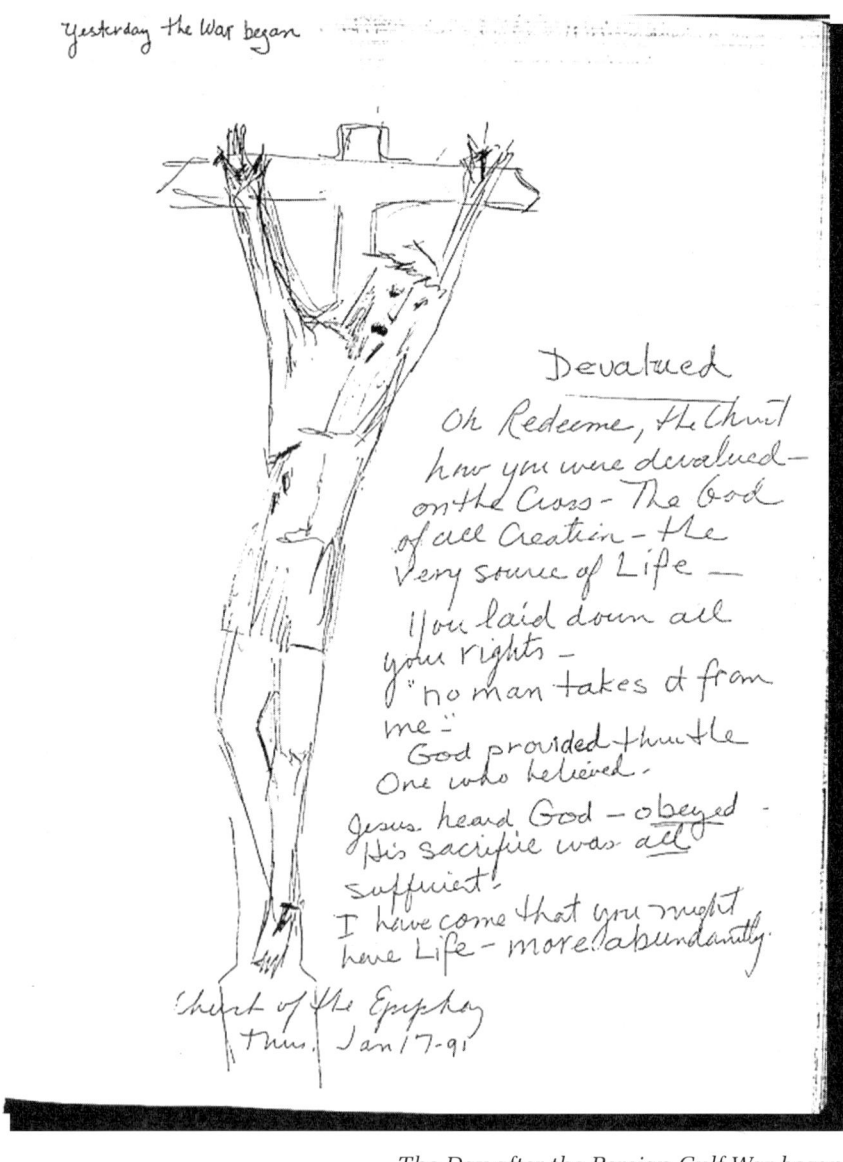

> Devalued
>
> Oh Redeemer, the Christ
> how you were devalued —
> on the Cross — The God
> of all Creation — the
> Very source of Life —
> You laid down all
> your rights —
> "no man takes it from
> me" —
> God provided thru the
> One who believed.
> Jesus heard God — obeyed —
> His sacrifice was *all*
> sufficient!
> I have come that you might
> have Life — more abundantly.
>
> Chapel of the Epiphany
> Thurs. Jan/7-91

The Day after the Persian Gulf War began

God disarmed the principalities and powers that were ranged against us and
made a bold display and public example of them,
in triumphing over them in Him and in the cross.

Colossians 2:15 AMP

HE LIVES!

HE LIVES is an excerpt from Pastor Thomas Severson's sermon to the Vineyard Christian Fellowship of Elgin, Illinois on Easter Sunday, April 4, 1999.

If there is ever a day for you to tune in, this is the day. Sometimes we put up deflector shields like in Star Trek, when the spaceship flew into a rain of asteroids. They put up an invisible shield that allowed everything to bounce off of it. We have a tendency to do that on religious days and with religious issues. We have the ability to look as if we are intently listening during a meeting or a sermon, when we are actually a thousand miles away.

But today I want to encourage you—as Jesus said—to have ears to hear what God is saying because the resurrection can make all the difference in the world. If you have the news that Christ is risen, it does not matter what other things you are facing in your life. After Christ's death, the disciples experienced an absolutely abysmal depression and they gave up on life. They had lost everything. All that Jesus had taught them in three-and-a-half years, suddenly dribbled away to nothing. But after the resurrection, they became little Christs themselves; that is what the word "Christian" means. These same disciples turned the world upside down and changed the course of human history through the hope and power of the resurrection. That same opportunity and invitation is here for us today.

I do want to address one thing up front: the resurrection happened. There are Christians who will debate the resurrection any time and any place. There are some in this church who have researched the facts and studied them. But for those who may want to hear the facts, let me go over a few things from Ravi Zacharias' research in *Can Man Live Without God*.

1. Jesus Christ Himself talked of his resurrection on repeated occasions. Both His enemies and His followers were told to expect it. Those who sought to smother His teaching took elaborate steps to counter the possibility of His claim, including the placement of a Roman guard at the door to the tomb.

2. Although His supporters basically understood His promise to rise from the dead and had even witnessed His raising of Lazarus, they did not really believe that He meant it literally until after the fact. Therefore, they could not be accused of creating the scenario for this deception.

3. It was the post-resurrection appearance that made the ultimate difference to the skeptical mind of Thomas and the resistant will of Paul.

From Ravi Zacharias, *Can Man Live Without God* (Word Publishing, Nashville, TN, ©1994. All Rights reserved), 162-163, by permission of the publisher.

4. The transformation of His disciples from a terrified bunch of individuals who felt themselves betrayed into a fearless group ready to proclaim the message to Rome and to the rest of the world cannot be explained with a mere shrug of the shoulder.

5. Had the Roman authorities wanted to eradicate Jesus' teaching once and for all, they would have only needed to present His dead body—but they could not. There is something often missed here. If the disciples were fabricators of an ideal, they could have been merely posited in a spiritual resurrection, which could have been done even with the presence of a dead body. Instead, they went the hard way, by talking of the resurrection of the actual physical body, which, if not true, was an enormous risk to take should the body have ever been detected. No, they believed in a literal resurrection because they had witnessed it. This is a very telling piece of evidence in light of the fact that Rome, itself, once diametrically opposed to the gospel, was later won over to Jesus' message. The religious leaders wanted nothing more than they wanted to stifle Christianity. And in fact, Jesus' own brother James was not a believer until after the resurrection.

6. One other very interesting factor to bring to our attention is from non-Christian sources. Even the Koran, which is hardly in favor of the Christian message, attests to Jesus' virgin birth and credits Him with the unique power to raise the dead, a most interesting notation often forgotten by the Muslims themselves.

Let's look beyond the historical fact of the resurrection to Paul's summary of the events of Jesus' death, burial, and resurrection. He says, "For I passed on to you—as among the first to hear it, the message I had myself received—that Christ died for our sins, as the scriptures said He would; that He was buried and rose again on the third day, again as the scriptures foretold. He was seen by Cephas, then by the twelve, and subsequently, He was seen by over five hundred Christians" (1 Cor. 15:3-6, Phillips).

Who is this Christ who died for our sins in accordance with the scriptures? If you measure Him by today's standards of success, whether in education, money, family, good looks, long life, or impressive career, Jesus Christ seems like a total failure. Although His virgin birth was miraculous, it left a bastard shadow over His life. He did not pursue any higher education. He worked as a carpenter, an itinerant preacher. He never travelled more than a few hundred miles from where he was born. He wasn't a rock star, an athlete, a political leader, or a famous general. He did have miraculous powers. He could heal. He could deliver. He raised several from the dead, but He totally lacked the sense of promotion and organization needed to build a ministry. He seemed crippled by an undiminished compassion and love for people. Apart from His relationship with God and His disciples, feeding people, washing feet, sharing the truth in love, grace and mercy, healing sick bodies and delivering oppressed people was ALL that He was about.

For his book, *What's So Amazing About Grace?*, Phillip Yancy did a study which found that people today generally dislike Christians and the church, but absolutely admire and love Jesus Christ. As a pastor, I wonder about the disparity between who Jesus was and who the church is. It gives us something to think about. Christ said, "No" to a political career; He said, "No" to vengeance on His enemies. However, He said, "Yes" to love and forgiveness; He said, "Yes" to the cross. He seemed to have a death wish for the cross, a destiny and a determination to get to the cross which accelerated his rapid downward mobility. Besides being the worst form of torturous execution that human kind had ever invented, the cross was strictly a criminal's death.

Consider Jesus through the lens of American success. He was born in a stable and crucified with criminals. He had no currency to speak of, only compassion. He was not popular with the people, but He possessed the Father's love. He had no fame on earth, just a name in heaven. He had one mission and one purpose on earth: to seek and save that which was lost. When Adam and Eve obeyed the serpent in the garden, they lost Paradise; it was regained when Christ obeyed His Father in a garden. He literally became sin's penalty and man's redeemer, separated from His Father, so that He could break the satanic grip on mankind's heart.

I think the challenge to our unbelief occurred at His death and after His death. Christ died for our sins in accordance with the scriptures. As I was studying the word, it was painful to see that after His resurrection, Jesus had to reprove His disciples for their unbelief. In fact, if you read a gospel in one sitting, it is amazing to note that Jesus' primary challenge is not to unbelievers but to His church for their lack of faith. His message was essentially, "How can you be upset about this and worried about that, when I am the resurrection and the life, and I have overcome sin, hell, and death? He still asks the same things of us: "How can you allow a grade on a paper, a promotion that didn't go your way, or a disruption in your family situation to cave in your world, when I am the life, I am the truth, and I am the way?"

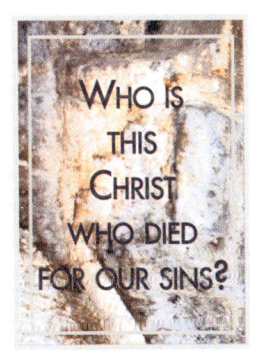

When Christ was buried and the tomb was sealed, the religious world breathed a sigh of relief. There would be no more disruptions of the status quo and no more embarrassing questions They could stop searching for the perfect plan to trap and embarrass Jesus only to have it backfire on them. All those days were over. They paid the gold pieces to have Him betrayed, and they got what they wanted, Christ in the grave. Even the political world breathed a sigh of relief when Christ was put in the tomb. There would be no more killing of all the babies under a certain age, no more chasing Him down, no more worrying that the scriptures about a Messiah were actually talking about a political leader. Finally, the demonic world breathed a sigh of relief when Christ was put in the tomb, for how could a dead man-god save, heal, and deliver or feed people any more? His operation was totally shut down. As the religious, political, and demonic worlds smiled, Christ's disciples slumped into hiding and depression. Not only had they lost their master, their teacher, and their best friend, but His words of instruction to them had lost credibility. Words like "Whosoever desires to come after Me let him deny himself, take up his cross, and follow Me. For whoever desires to save his life will lose it, but whoever loses His life for my sake and the gospel's will save it,"[1] seemed pretty impossible. They cowered in fear from the authorities, and didn't want to face the cross.

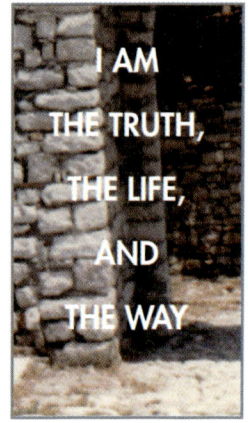

Now I submit to you that if the story had ended on this note, Christianity would never have existed. You couldn't find a history book with the name of Jesus Christ in it, and we would not be sitting here today celebrating Easter. But the story didn't end at the sealed tomb. You might say that a funny thing happened on the way to decomposition, for He rose again on the third day in accordance with the scriptures. Jesus Christ was raised from the dead by the resurrection power of the Father. The One who had stooped so low in obedience and death on the cross was now highly exalted over every name in Heaven. The good guy had won. The poor in spirit got the kingdom of heaven. The one who mourned at the cross was comforted by His Father, and the meek one, the sacrificial lamb, inherited the earth. The one who had hungered and thirsted after righteousness was filled. The one who forgave sins freely was raised up by His Father. The one who was pure in heart saw God. The one who was persecuted for righteousness' sake got the Kingdom of Heaven. The peacemaker lived as God's firstborn son. Christ's addiction to the Father's

---

1. Mark 8:34 NKJV

will and the Father's glory, His gambling of His life away with the hope of winning ours was gloriously rewarded. Death was defeated and Paradise regained. Christ was now the firstborn of many brethren who will follow on the path prepared for them.

The religious world, the political world, and the demonic world were absolutely stunned because as long as His disciples believe in the resurrection, the Kingdom of God will advance in power and glory. The opposing forces had only one choice—to give up ground. Christ is risen and "Jesus is the Victor!" becomes the cry of the human heart that is ready to acknowledge God's ability to forgive any sin. He restores anyone to the Father, releasing His kingdom, His Holy Spirit, His goodness, His kindness, His joy, and His peace. The message comes in power to the "guttermost," the "uttermost," and everyone in-between.

When the human race sinned in the garden, you, me, Adam, Eve, and everyone in-between needed divine pardon. All of the world's religions and the world's finest men could not bring us back to the garden again. The two enemies that Christ soundly defeated were sin and death. We need Christ because He is the only one who has defeated death, and He is the only one who can change a sinful heart, one that has been separated from God. He can enter it internally, rewire it and connect it to the life and peace of God. I've heard someone say, "Confucius: tomb occupied, Buddha: tomb occupied. Mohammed: tomb occupied." Nice guys, but they ran up against sin and death. You and I won't do any better. We won't do any better apart from Christ. But with Christ? TOMB EMPTY.

The Empty Tomb, Jerusalem

3 Union With Him

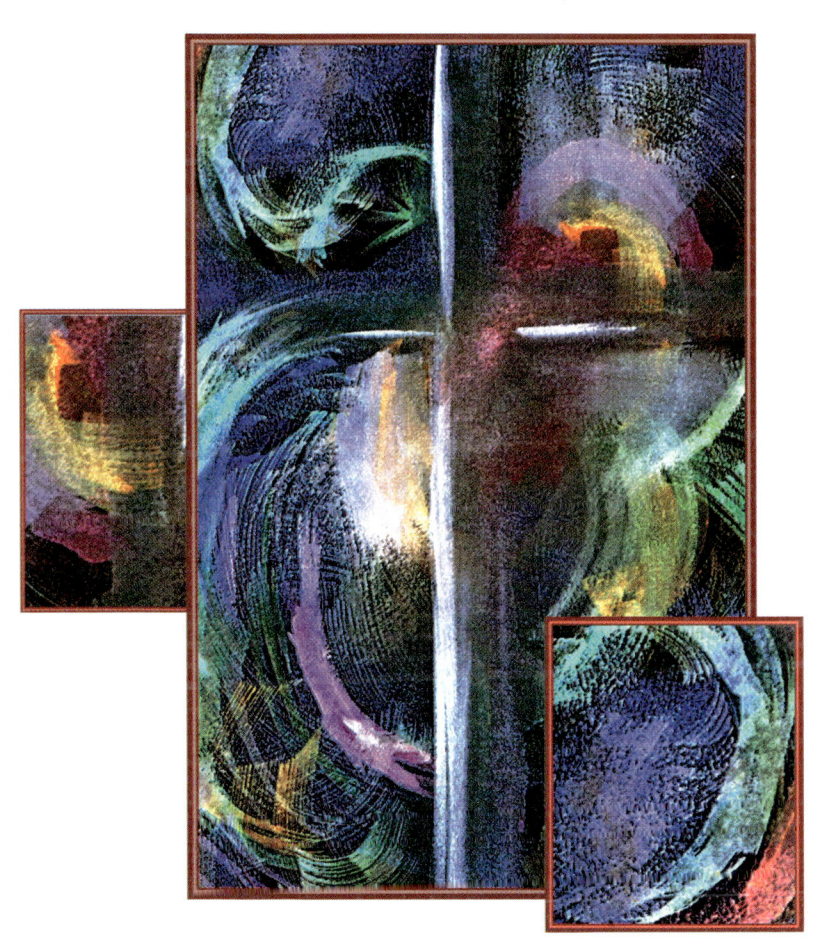

One died for all, therefore all died; and He died for all,
that they who live should no longer live for themselves,
but for Him who died.

2 Corinthians 5:14-15 NASB

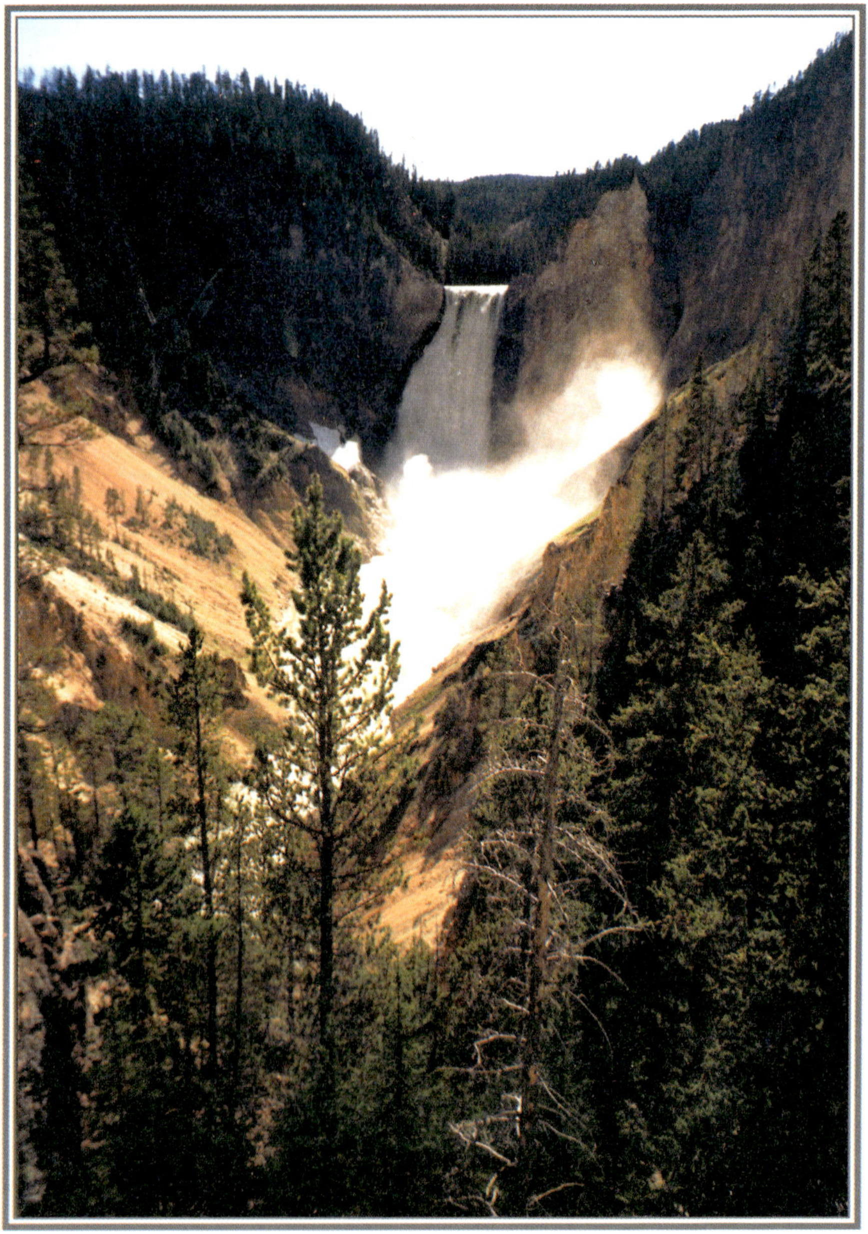

JUST FOR YOU

I pour out my heart: I love You, I love to speak of You.
Your name is like honey on my lips. I love to speak Your name
You are the innocence in me. You are the wisdom in me. You are the purity in me.
You are the unconditional surrender of love in me.
You are the abounding joy which bubbles in my soul.
You are the light that beams from my eyes.
You are the very essence of the holiness I long for.
You are my every thought. You are my every breath. I adore You.
You are the laughter from which my smile explodes.
You are the aura of peace which rests around me.
You are my precious pearl that I would give up my life to hold onto.
You are the desire of my heart. You are the delight of my body, soul, and spirit.
You are the place in which I hide. You are the arms into which I fall.
You are the shadow which covers me.
You are the source from which my strength exists.
You are the Guide which never lets go of my hand.
You are the Friend who understands the very deep cravings of my soul.
You are the motivation which drives me forward.
You are the attraction which holds me in Your world.
You are the distraction which sets me apart.
You are the hunger that binds me to Your table.
You are the water which never runs dry.
You are the Eternal Lover who has captured my heart.
You are the power which has delivered me from death.
You are the miracle which has set me free. You are the air in which I fly.
You are the wind beneath my wings.
You are the heartbeat which sustains my existence.
You are my Creator who holds my universe in place.
You are my Savior who rescued me from tragedy.
You are my redeemer who has replaced my past.
You are my Master to whom I am a willing slave.
I surrender to anything You will to do with me.
I beg to sit at Your feet serving You endlessly.
You are my Lord who controls my every move.
You are my Protector who keeps me safe from harm.
You are my Father who gives up all that is Precious to have me as Your daughter.
You are my Comforter who will never leave me or forsake me no matter what occurs.
You are the Presence which refreshes my soul. You are the Lover of my soul.
You are Life to me. You are Truth to me. You are the only Way I choose to go.
You are the Victorious Spirit which sustains my life.
You are the Glory which draws me into audience with You.
You are the River of Life which never fails. You are the Flood which refreshes
   my soul in the secret place where You await me every day.

As one act of sin exposed the whole race of men to God's judgment and condemnation,
so one act of perfect righteousness presents all men freely acquitted in the sight of God.

Romans 5:18 Phillips

WE BELIEVE

We believe He died
In love with you and me.
Yielded, determined, and unafraid
To hang upon a shame cursed tree.

We believe He took our guilt.
He bore our grief, our pain, our sin.
He took our selfish flesh to die
Upon that cross of love with Him.

We believe He lives.
He reigns, omnipotent, and free
Full of joy His Spirit comes
Giving Life to you and me.

A HUGE LESSON

C. S. Kellough (Used by permission)

Twenty years ago, all the people I walked with knew about "taking the cross." Because they'd grown up with the message and had known it all their lives, they assumed everyone who came into Christ could "take the cross" too. I couldn't. But because of their familiarity with the message, they couldn't communicate any practical applications to help me, and they had no idea of how to teach me to do it.

Because I didn't have the slightest idea of how to "take it to the cross," I'd been pleading with the Lord, "Oh, Lord, I really want this crucified life. I want to live so that it's no longer I who lives but Christ who lives in me" (Galatians 2:20). I didn't want the crucified life for any big glory reasons; I wanted the victory Jesus had and I didn't. I knew it was wrong to say by faith that I was crucified with Christ when I was acting another way. I could have said it 9,000 times, and it wouldn't have made a difference because that wasn't where it was. Some think that's where the crucified life is, but it isn't. I wanted to be good and grow, but sometimes, when someone would hit me with their words, I did what I didn't want to do. I'd criticize. At other times, I'd be worn out or the kids would act up, and I'd yell "Shut up" or a profanity.

Why did I do it? The Holy Ghost was convicting me of my own person. I did not want my ugly self. I did not want to displease my Father who loved me so much that He sent His Son to die for me. It was a time of seeking. I'd sit down and weep and say, "Lord, I know there's something more. I know it." I had the thirst, but not the wherewithal. I felt two-faced. I could be good for a little while, then I'd do something yucko. I'd cry, "Lord, I'm like Paul. I keep on doing what I don't want to do. Lord! It's me that lives, not you. I need to die!" (Romans 7:19) The Lord was waiting. He had a plan, a divine setup, to deal with the intensity of my flesh.

Many years ago, when a beloved child was about fourteen and absolutely the neatest kid in the world—good looking, smart, all that kind of stuff—the child developed a potentially fatal condition. The family went to doctors. They prayed. They prayed alone, they prayed together, and they had other people pray. They tried deliverance and this beloved child was in full agreement with it. They did everything available to do and nothing helped. When things seemed to be getting better, they would get worse. It was an impossible situation; this precious child was having a tremendously difficult time, and it was just tearing me apart. I dearly treasure children and this one was like gold to me.

One particular evening after supper, while I was washing the dishes and praising the Lord, I heard sounds that indicated a difficulty coming from upstairs in the far end of the house. Immediately I screamed, commanding loudly, "In the name of Jesus Christ and the power of His blood, Satan, stop it! Leave this child alone!" I tore through the house; it was a long way through the sprawled out farm house. When I went to the bottom of the stairs to go to the child, someone else was sitting in the living room at the bottom of the stairs. This person, listening to the accuser of the brethren, said, "Well, if this child would have ever had any kind of an example, this never would have happened." Well let me tell you, I've got English on one side and wild Irish blood on the other. Every drop of Irish nature ran to the surface. This hit the nerve in my flesh that released vengeance without mercy. I wanted to annihilate the person who had said those words. They were the farthest thing from the truth. I knew all that had been done for this particular child. I wanted to put blame where I thought it deserved to go. Talk about hatred and self-righteousness. I felt the destructive passion rising; everything wild arose within my flesh. I felt the blasphemy and cursing come. I felt the hatred come. Murder was in my eyes; hatred was in my flesh. I wanted to get even. There was a fullness of destruction within me, and I had the ability to let it come out of my mouth and hands.

Now as I've said, for about a year I'd been asking, "Lord, teach me how to walk the cross. I need to have revelation of the cross." At the very moment of intensity as the fullness of my flesh came to the surface, I hit my fist and was in my trap. The power of the Holy Ghost twirled me around and I ran to the back of the house to a milk shed door that was shaped like a cross. I threw myself against that cross and cried, "Lord! Take the mean me out of me! Lord, take it! Take me on the cross! I choose the cross of Jesus Christ! I choose the cross of Jesus Christ and not myself!"

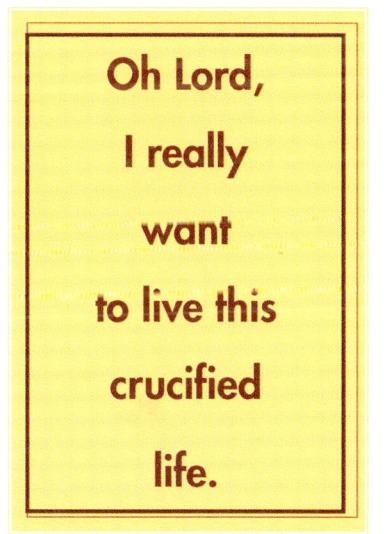

> **Oh Lord, I really want to live this crucified life.**

As I hung there for a time repeating, "I choose the cross. I choose the cross. I'm in You on the cross," the meanness of countless generations suddenly fell away. All the anger drained out of me. Every tainted motive, all the disrespect, resentment, bitterness, violence, and stored up hatred, every feeling of being short changed, every intense feeling that rises in response to abuse was gone, everything that flesh wants to talk about drained out on the cross of Jesus Christ, never again to return, even twenty years later.

I turned around, walked back to the kitchen, and finished doing the dishes full of absolute peace, a peace from heaven. The house was filled with peace, as though nothing had happened. I didn't even really think of it again.

About three days later I realized that this beloved child had been healed. At the very minute the Holy Spirit had hurled me to the cross, a precious one was totally, instantly, miraculously taken to the resurrection side of the cross of Jesus Christ and healed. In the miracle working power of the other side of the cross, this child has never again had the first symptom. Today, I doubt there remains any memory of that awful time or if the child, who is now fully grown, truly realizes that it ever happened. And glory to glory, some things that were embedded in my flesh are gone.

I couldn't choose the cross. I didn't know how. My passion was too great to "just take it to the cross." Resignation will never make a situation go away. Only the cross can take care of our moral situations, our utter failures. God answered my prayer and took me to the cross. In taking me there, He taught me how to take the cross. God started me with a huge lesson, not a small one. He gave me a huge experience of resurrection power, of coming through the cross, of believing, and of joy. The joy of the wonderful walk of this particular child might never have reached its fullness. It came through the grace of God at the cross. It is joy unspeakable and full of glory, full of glory, full of glory,[1] and the fullness has not yet been known.

---

1. The line "It is joy unspeakable and full of glory, full of glory, full of glory" is from the chorus of the hymn, *Joy Unspeakable,* words and music written by B.E. Warren.

"Our Father"
Proverbs 4:20-22

COME UNTO ME

Caught in a world where it's hard to be free—
    Jesus calls softly,
        "Come, follow Me."

Here in the middle of sin and of strife—
    Jesus calls softly,
        "Come, live My life."

Amidst all the struggles that pull from each side—
    Jesus calls softly,
        "Come be My Bride."

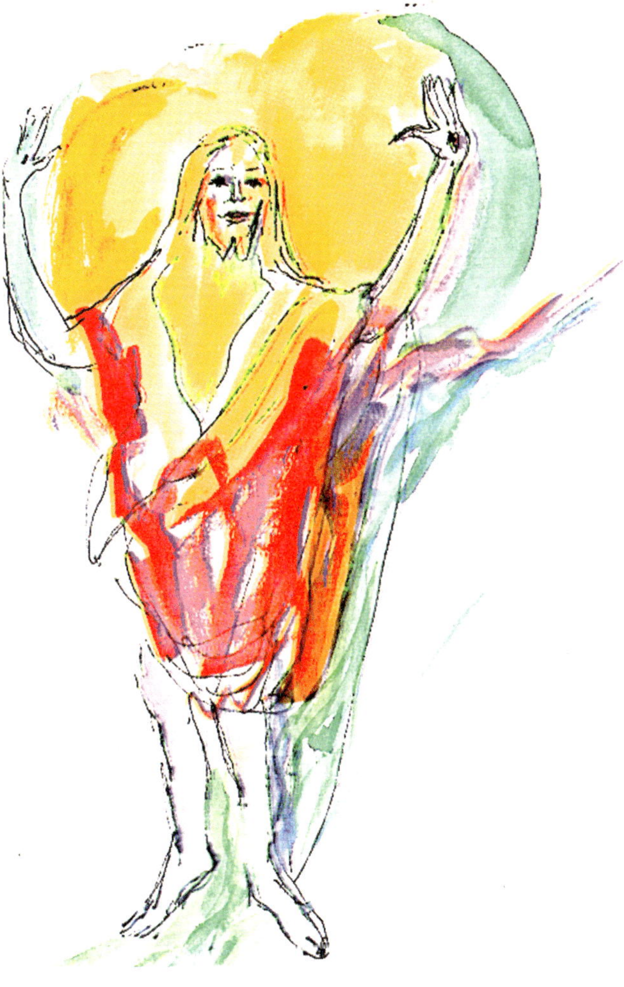

FOLLOWING HIS FOOTSTEPS

When I gave my heart to the Lord many years ago, I was struggling in an unhappy marriage. I could not seem to fix it, so I finally surrendered it to Jesus. I told Him that if He wanted my broken heart, He could have it—and the marriage too. As soon as I turned my gaze toward Him, Jesus began to reconstruct my life.

As a youth, I grew up seeing images of a suffering Jesus. He was always on the cross, so I expected life on earth to be painful. In the midst of every marital difficulty, I had concluded that my only choice was to silently endure any mistreatment. Instead, the Holy Spirit began instructing me about new methods of handling our problems. When an angry blow-up with my husband arouse and bitter words were spoken, I went into another room and asked Jesus to give me His way of dealing with the hostility.

Almost immediately, I felt the peaceful presence of the Holy Spirit in my heart, as if He were giving me an alternative battle plan. Instead of responding harshly, I was able to trust Him to release His words through me! When I returned to my husband and spoke kind thoughts, he was suddenly disarmed and speechless. The skirmish disintegrated; peace was temporarily restored.

Eventually I was introduced to a teaching that claimed I did not have to suffer because Jesus had suffered for me on the cross. I heartily agreed with that theology and gleefully destroyed every book in my personal library that even mentioned the word "suffering." Instead of always expecting pain, I decided that I would never have to experience pain again. I saw only two choices—always or never. I did not see that suffering and release from suffering are both sides of the same cross. In between the two lies death.

I was caught in the middle of a lie because my marriage had not permanently improved, but now I was unable to talk about it, for any negative words were called "bad confessions." If I believed that everything was supposed to be good, I had to pretend that the ugly part of my life did not exist—but my fairytale kingdom was about to be invaded by the Holy Spirit of Truth.

When our prayer group began studying a book about biblical mercy,[1] I felt like I had enrolled in a foreign language school because the concepts were so

---

1. *What the Bible Teaches about Mercy* by Rex Andrews, ©1985, Zion Faith Homes, Zion, Illinois 60099

new to me. I had no understanding of what true mercy was or how it should be applied. When I wanted to suffer, mercy was not really welcome; when I lived in fantasy land, mercy was not needed.

Instead, I discovered that God is full of mercy AND justice, but His justice requires that I must be honest about my situation. He knows the real condition of my heart and if I am guilty or in pain, I have to admit it. Otherwise I do not need His merciful intervention. My marriage was really in trouble and I needed to see it from His perspective.

For the first time, I began to realize that God's warnings are an invitation to change. If I am in sin, He gives me a choice: either I accept the truth and repent, or I refuse His offer of grace and receive chastisement. One act of God produces either mercy or judgment, depending on how I respond to His commands.

The Lord mercifully allows pain to get our attention and turn our lives back from permanent destruction. In His loving hands, there is a good solution to every situation. If He must wound us, He promises to heal us. Meanwhile, the problems in my marriage escalated until they reached a crisis point. Through a prophetic word, the Lord told me that something I'd been carrying for a long time was now over and that He was going to handle it Himself. I immediately rejoiced, because I assumed that my marriage would be dramatically healed by a miraculous intervention.

To my surprise, after a few days I felt the Lord talking directly to my heart. Yes, He intended to change the situation, but He wanted to do it through me. He had heard my prayers and tears; it was time to act. He asked me to give my husband a warning, as if I were Moses dealing with Pharaoh. I could no longer be afraid and silent in the midst of the abuse. The Lord asked me to be His voice and address the issues. When I told my husband that we could no longer cover up the abuse and that we had to face the truth, he denied the problems. God's offer to extend mercy was refused and judgment began.

Eventually, I obtained a legal separation and the children and I left the house. Many miraculous doors opened as we followed the Lord to our new place. He even provided men from the church to move us the very day after I asked for help. Everywhere I turned, I saw His faithfulness surrounding us.

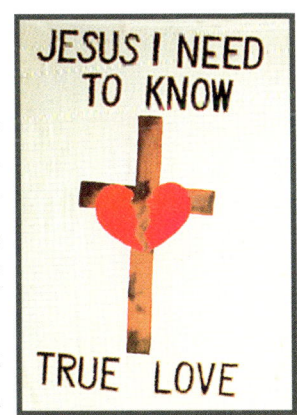

About three months later, I had a dream that allowed me to see my part in the sinful situation. In it, my husband and I arrived at a house and I watched as the owners were murdered. I did not try to stop it, and I did not go for help. As we left the house together, I accidentally set off an alarm system. When we realized that the police had been notified, we both fled to a nearby stadium to get lost in the crowd.

Eventually, I decided to turn myself in and went to the authorities. I was immediately taken to the precinct office and there I saw a line of friends and family who had come to help. My heavenly Father was there and He had been crying. Jesus was there too, and He was still crying. Then I turned to stand before the Holy Spirit. He gently but firmly took my face in His hands and said directly to me, "This is going to be hard for you, but you must go to prison for a season." I was calm and completely at peace because I knew that He was doing it for my own good. I could trust His decree of justice.

When I awoke, I was crying about my sin of passivity. I realized that I needed a time of confinement and rehabilitation. Then I understood that I was already in a type of minimum-security prison because I was away from my husband and home. In that place of safety, I could learn to express emotions like joy and anger that I had stifled in the presence of rage. I also began to express new ways of worship through dancing as I experienced the wonders of the Father's love for me. At the same time, I saw many positive changes in the children as we started rebuilding our relationships. Above all, I learned how to confront sin as a means of expressing true love. I stopped retreating in the face of opposition.

I had read many verses that described men's plots to capture and kill Jesus. Sometimes He openly addressed their hatred, and sometimes He walked silently away from their accusations. He was able to do both because He did and said only what He saw and heard His Father doing. However, when He heard His Father tell Him to go the the cross, He died. He did not allow men to take His life; He willingly gave it as an act of instant obedience. In contrast, I let someone take my joy, my peace, my hopes, and my dreams and I expected God to be pleased with those sacrifices. That is not obedience. He wants my relationship with Him to be so secure, that He can tell me His desires and I will instantly obey.

After I had been separated for a year and a half, I felt the Lord's encouragement to move to another town and pursue a Master's degree in education. I had been out of school for twenty years, but that didn't make any difference to Him. Since one of my children had graduated from a local university and the other one was going away to college, He opened a new door of adventure for me. I had a delightful time getting my degree and student teaching, but He also required me to continue taking a tough stand with my husband.

I had no idea when I began addressing the issues how long the process would be before the problems would be solved. In fact, the Lord never promised me that we definitely would be reconciled. He told me that there would be no more abuse and that my latter years would be greater than my former years, but I did not know for certain if I would spend those remaining years alone. When everything looked hopeless, I still believed that the Lord's goodness wanted to draw my husband to a place of repentance.

After he suffered some very painful losses and was ready to hear the truth, we began talking with a marriage counselor. In the meantime, the actual home that we had built was sold; then it was torn down to make way for someone else's new construction project. Its physical destruction painted a vivid picture of what the Lord had done to our marriage. Our labors had been in vain because we followed our own individual blueprints for a "godly" marriage. He literally and figuratively demolished what we had built and then asked us to join His construction crew.

Today, the Lord is building a new home from our converted hearts. He is using His own materials, following His specifications, and laying His foundation upon the completed work of His Son, Jesus. All He requires from us is that we cooperate with Him. As we follow Him, He will build the house of His dreams, a solid structure that will survive any storm that may come our way.

*For I know the thoughts that I think toward you,
says the Lord, thoughts of peace and not of evil,
to give you a future and a hope.*

Jeremiah 29:11

REPENTANCE

Disgusted, just disgusted
As I look and see my sin.
And then, with pomp and dignity,
I do it all again.

I, like Paul, would hate the thing
I find I always do.
I cry out and ask for grace
To see this journey through.

Keep my eyes upon the cross,
Upon the blood of Him
Who paid the payment, set me free,
And gave me power to win.

Iron grate to protect tourists from falling into a cave where ancient Israelites hid from invading enemies

EYES MEET

Quiet eyes,
No fear or angry demon
Peering through,
No ripple of anxiety
No haze of doubt in You.

Quiet eyes,
Immeasurable
Oceans of rest,
Endless energy
Free from stress.

Quiet eyes
Of covenant trust
Pour Your Abba's
Love on us.

Quiet eyes
Blaze forth
No force can escape
Your scorching.

Quiet eyes
Condense
in focused power.
Draw me close
To watch with You
This final hour.

Abigail Apon, age 10

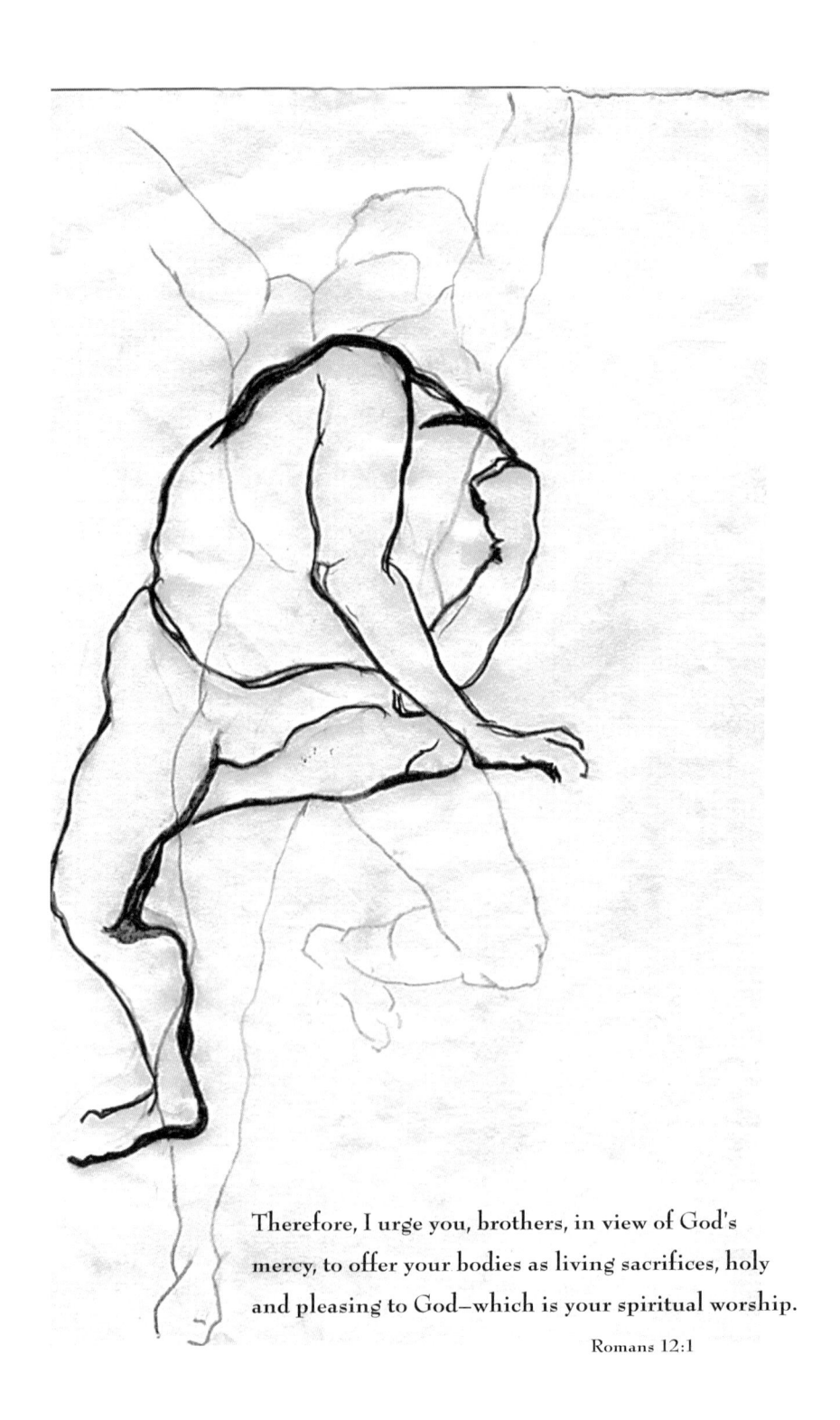

Therefore, I urge you, brothers, in view of God's mercy, to offer your bodies as living sacrifices, holy and pleasing to God—which is your spiritual worship.

Romans 12:1

Sweeter than dead dreams
And self's desires,
All consuming
YOU burn within me.
Burn, Lord, burn.
Consume me, Lord.
Let Your Fire,
Pure, Holy Fire,
Lift sweet odors
As You seize my heart
And hold it,
Flaming,
On the altar of Your love,
That I, too, like You,
May be
Burnt offering,
Acceptable sacrifice
Unto God.

IN LOVE

Gray haired and wrinkled,
I still scan the heavens—
Search within Your Word,
And seek to see Your glory.
I long for Your appearing,
Listen for Your singing in my heart,
And find Your imprint everywhere.

Send more love to soften
Reluctant corners in my soul.
Fuel Your fires within me
To a white hot glow
For the older I grow
The more I know that love obeys
In extravagant ways—

I need Your Life,
Not mine, at the core.
Don't let me cling
To earthly things.
Give me joyful grace
To bring all age and loss into Your cross.

Decades ago I read John Donne
"Batter my heart You Three Personed God."
You've battered it, shattered it
and put it together again—
Keep wrestling with me Most Holy God
Until You win.

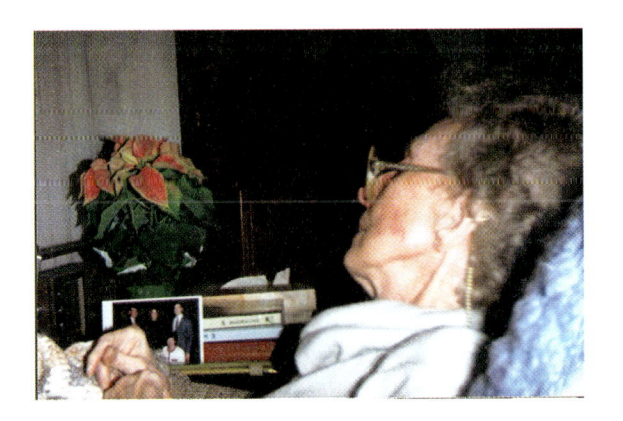

SHOW US

Truth, Mercy and Light
Love, Majesty and Might
Creator of all the earth
You came to show us our worth
And make us holy in Your sight.

We are lowly and weak
Slow to turn the other cheek
You showed us how to forgive
and die to self in order to live
And serve, being humble and meek

Show us what You have done
Protect us from the evil one
Make Your victory real today
Show us how we should pray
And be a reflection of Your shining Son.

Jesus is the brightness of God's glory and the exact representation of God's very being. He upholds all things by the word of His power. When He had by Himself purged our sins, He sat down on the right hand of the Majesty on high.

Hebrews 1:3 Adapted from KJV and Rotterham

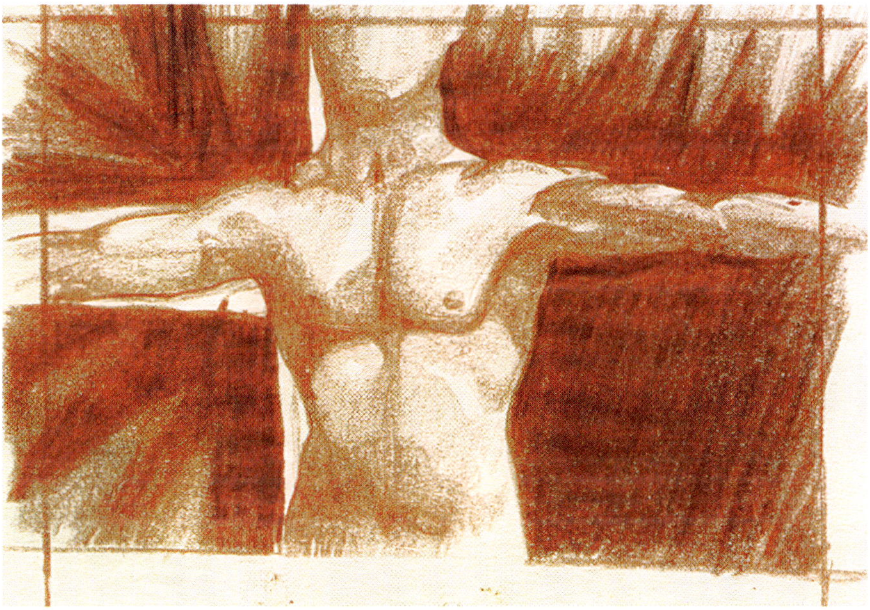

HUMAN WEAKNESS
AND THE POWER OF GOD

Michael Sullivant
Metro Christian Fellowship of Kansas City, Missouri 7/11/98

Make the Word of God alive to us today. Father we appeal to You. Help us. Let our hearts be fertile soil, that good soil that receives the seed of the Word of God and brings forth fruit in time. May that be true of our lives. In the name of Jesus, we ask it.

The Lord wants to bring forth a higher caliber of the prophetic ministry of the Holy Spirit in the body of Christ. It is important to understand what that involves and to begin to aim for it, to search after it, and not to be content with past levels. In every increase of prophetic caliber there will be a dynamic of death and resurrection. The Lord showed this to a prophetic brother in a very clear vision. He saw different calibers of rifles representing different levels of prophetic experience. God would release and establish a certain caliber of the prophetic experience. Then the prophetic would die and be resurrected into the next higher caliber. The increase was related to the quality of our human life as Spirit filled believers before the Lord.

Increase in caliber ties into the message of the cross, the ministry of the cross. Understanding the ministry of the cross of Jesus is critically important to the church. The cross is the most profound act that human history has ever known. It's the most important thing that the universe has ever experienced. God became human and died on the cross. In His death and resurrection is the key to understanding what life in God's kingdom, life under God, is all about. If our Christianity is crossless, then our Christianity is going to be counterfeit, weak and futile. The cross is not a one time experience. A rhythm of death and resurrection continues throughout our Christian lives. We never outgrow the applications of the cross. God always brings us back to further and deeper applications of the life of the cross, the meaning of the cross, the message of the cross.

> The secret is a revelation of the cross.

Some years ago I had a very intense spiritual dream. In it, the Lord was giving a refined and purified faith to the body of Christ. It came out of intimacy with the Lord, an intimacy with the Holy Spirit who was revealing the will of God to Spirit filled believers. As we discerned the will of God, we had the same experience that Jesus had when He saw what the Father was doing in Heaven and then, in specific situations, He accomplished it on earth. We were anointed with the prophetic power that flowed out of intimacy with the Holy Spirit. We didn't go off on our own, in our own wishes and desires, commanding things to happen. Power was for ministry, not to get wealthy.

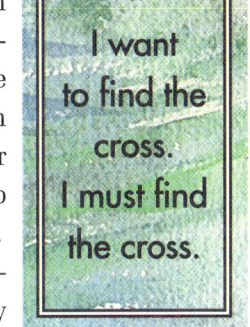

As we saw things on earth, we weren't panicked. We weren't hyped up. It was a very lovely experience. We simply saw things in heaven. We knew the heart of God, and we knew what God wanted. We were almost shocked when we saw things on earth that didn't agree with the things in Heaven. When we ran into situations that we knew were contrary to the will of God, we thought, "Well, that's not the way that's supposed to be because I saw something different in this situation in Heaven. God wants something different here. Then we simply pointed at those situations and said, "In the name of Jesus, change," and they changed.

Standing in a heavenly place, I saw a scene with the cross of Jesus in it. The cross represented the purpose and the presence of God. Then I was whisked back down to earth and I saw the exact same scene, but I couldn't find the cross. I knew it was there, hidden like objects in the hidden pictures of *Highlights for Children* magazines. I didn't know where it was, but I went on a search for it. I was on a search for the presence and the purpose of God. I remember taking the first step. I hesitated just for a moment as I realized that if I found the cross, I could lose my life. I might be a martyr. I quickly realized the cost facing me. Suddenly such a resolute, passionate, overwhelming love for the presence and the purpose of God rushed into my spirit that I don't have words to describe it to you. I realized that I might die, but it didn't matter. As I hesitated, I said, "I might die," but then I said, "I don't care. I need the presence of God. I need the purpose of God. That's what my life is about. I may die in the process but it doesn't matter. I want to find the cross. I must find the cross. It is my purpose. It is my meaning. It is what gives meaning to my human existence. I must find the cross. And if I die in the process, so be it." I counted the cost, very quickly added it up, and said that it was meaningless in comparison to the cross. Like Paul, I saw that all of my human accolades, all of my human accomplishments, all of the things that I have done on my own apart from intimacy with God don't count for anything. They are dung compared to the excellency of being intimate with Jesus Christ. I had to find the cross and embrace it.

> We are designed to be disciples.

Then I went on a joyful journey, a joyful adventure to find the hidden cross in that scene. When I found it, I was so happy that I turned to my companion and rejoiced, "I found it. Here it is. I knew it was here." Then I wondered, "What's going to happen now? Maybe we'll die—but I found it!" It was very satisfying. Once again, I can't describe the feelings. I have never felt them in my actual experience. I pray someday I will. I pray that you will too, because they were completely satisfying, very, very moving, very profound and overwhelming. I felt like I understood the meaning of human existence.

This prophetic caliber of ministry comes from intimacy with the Holy Spirit and revolves around the dynamic of embracing the cross of Jesus. In First Corinthians 1:18 Paul says, "The message of the cross is foolishness to those who are perishing, but to us who are being saved it is the power of God." This life that we're called into, the lifestyle of embracing the cross, is foolishness to the world. This is a mystery and a paradox.

With His wisdom,.God challenges the value systems of mankind. Man says the cross is foolishness. God says the cross is the wisdom and power of God. If we embrace the cross, if we preach the cross, and if we live the cross, we will bear a stigma. We will bear a mark, a charge from the carnal mind of carnal people which says, "You're stupid for laying down your rights as a human being. You're stupid for giving away your life for someone else." After charging us with that, they'll say, "You're proud. You think you can be like Jesus. You're just proud." The irony of the stigma that we bear as Christians is that the message of the cross is the complete opposite of foolishness and pride. It is wisdom and it is humility. The essence of the wisdom is that God has designed my life to thrive when I yield all my rights to Him. I'm most happy when I understand that my life is hidden with Christ in God. It's the secret of my identity. I get there by embracing the cross, laying down my rights, yielding myself to my Master. We are built to be followers. We are designed to be disciples. We have not been designed to be autonomous gods unto ourselves.

When people try to be their own gods, they get stressed out. It's a big role to fill, especially when you're not omnipresent, omniscient, and omnipotent. Some of us have tried to be our own god and it was a hard job. The carnal mind says, "You're proud to think you're going to be like Jesus," but humility says, "I MUST be like Jesus. I MUST become like Him. I MUST empty myself so that I can become like Him." It is the supreme act of humility for human beings to say we must become like Jesus. The message of the cross is profound—the cross of Jesus Christ answers all the deepest longings of the human experience, all the deepest longings of the human heart.

I think the cross answers all human longings in three ways. The cross answers all the problems of guilt, of pain and injustice, and of the need for personal transformation. As much as people like to pretend they are not guilty, they are. We are born into this world with guilt because of the sin of our first parents. It's been passed on to us genetically and we've bought into it consciously and deliberately. We're guilty. The message of the cross answers the problem of human guilt. Every other religion and philosophy manipulates guilt feelings, but no other religion deals with guilt because only Jesus died for sins and satisfied the justice of God. Christianity is the only religion to squarely face the problem of guilt and give an answer. The Jews faced it, but now they don't have an answer because, in God's plan, temple sacrifices stopped in A.D. 70. We have an answer. We don't have to manipulate our guilt feelings. We don't have to pretend we're not guilty. We can just say: "OK, I am guilty. I've sinned." If you don't admit the disease and if you're in denial, then you won't take the medicine. Christ died for us. His death deals with the guilt and penalty of sin.

> **When people try to be their own gods, they get stressed out!**

The cross also deals with the pain of sin. In other words, it deals with the problem of injustice. At the cross, mercy and justice meet and kiss (Ps. 85:10). Love and faithfulness meet together; righteousness and peace kiss each other. In the cross we find mercy, but in the cross we also find justice because God dealt with sin on the cross. Jesus, the sinless Son of God, died on that cross. Even if you consider all the crimes, all of the millions of acts of injustice throughout human history, even the sins of other people against you that have almost destroyed your own lives—still, the greatest act of injustice ever to happen in the universe didn't happen to you. It didn't happen to a friend of yours. It happened to the Son of God when He who knew no sin was made sin for us (2 Cor. 5:21) and God killed Him. Did you know God killed Him? God executed Him on the cross for the sins of mankind. He laid the sins of mankind on Jesus. The sins of past generations and the sins of all future generations were somehow mysteriously laid on Jesus on the cross when He became sin. Talk about a mystery. How could God become Sin? But He did!

The cross deals with personal transformation and our longing for it. Not only did Christ die for us, but we died with Christ on the cross. It's a great paradox. In Galatians 2:20 Paul says, "I am crucified with Christ," or "I was crucified with Christ." What does that mean? It means Paul died with Christ. I am and I was executed with Christ. I died with Christ. I—my ego—died with Christ. "Nevertheless, I live." Now Paul, are you dead or are you alive? Yes I am crucified, but I'm alive, yet not I, but Christ lives in me. Paul keeps going back and forth. I'm dead, but I'm alive—but it's not me, it's Christ—but it is me, the life I now live. Now Paul, wait a minute. What are you talking about? Paul is talking about a mystery, a paradox. And we must let it touch us. We must drink it in. We must let it slap us around a little bit. "I'm dead, I'm alive. I'm dead, I'm alive. I feel like a spiritual schizophrenic." There are mysterious rhythms in the Kingdom of God. Healthy Christians should loosen up and learn to ride the waves of the paradoxes and mysteries of our faith. Galatians 2:20 is 220 current, double current. When you enter into its rhythm of death and life, you discover that you've been designed for God. You've been built to interface with God, and engage in His kingdom by a rhythm of death and resurrection. We need renewal, but we need something more radical than renewal. We need death and resurrection. Many Christians swoon rather than die; but swooners get resuscitated, not resurrected. Just Die!

I remember an experience when I was the pastor of a church. A man called and said, "I've got a gun and I'm going to kill myself. I'm the president of the gay liberation of Arkansas and Texas and I'm a psychologist and I'm going to kill myself unless you come and see me and talk to me—right now." I didn't know what to expect. I'd never met him and didn't know who he was. I looked over at him as I walked into his house, and I saw the spirit of death on him. He looked at me and said, "I want to kill myself." The power of the Lord came on me in a very wonderful way and I said, "You know, you need to die. But you don't need to kill yourself to die. Somebody else died for you and you mysteriously died with Him already, but you don't know it. That's the good news. You can die without killing yourself and have a new life. Do you want it?" He became a Christian that day.

We're called to the cross. Jesus said, "If anyone desires to come after Me, let him deny himself, and take up his cross daily and follow Me. For whoever desires to save his life will lose it, but whoever loses his life for My sake will save it"(Luke 9:23-4NKJV).

Are we to deny ourselves, or are we to fulfill ourselves? Which is it? Earlier this morning, I wrote a sentence about the paradox of self-denial and self-fulfillment:

When self-preservation is your first priority as a strategy for living, it is an inordinate desire and your self-fulfillment is being wrongly pursued, but when you sacrifice and subordinate self-fulfillment to following Jesus, it is a legitimate desire because you are wisely pursuing it.

The essence of the paradox is the desire for life God built into each of us. As Jesus asked, "What profit is it for a man to gain the whole world, and yet lose or forfeit his very self?" (Luke 9:25). What profit is it? Where's the payoff, the profit of human existence, if you gain the whole world but lose your soul? Self fulfillment, or self-actualization as some might call it, is a legitimate longing. God put it there, but the way to find it is mysterious.

> **Are we to deny ourselves or to fulfill ourselves?**

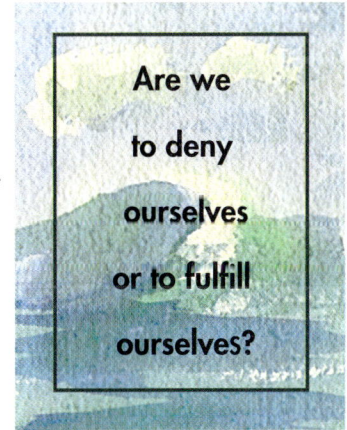

It's found by subordinating that desire, that passion for survival, to something greater and grander—to interface with Jesus, to follow Him, to be His disciple, to give your life away to Him. When you give your human life and all that you are—all of your time, your talents, and your treasures—and subordinate them to the Son of God who is your Master, you deny the preoccupation of fulfilling your life. Then in losing your life, you find it. Jesus is the Master, the genius of human life who knows life. He is a human today, exalted at the right hand of God. You are designed and built to be His follower, His disciple, His junior partner in the Kingdom of God by being a receptacle, a vessel of the Holy Spirit Himself. God lives inside of you.

Early this morning I believe the Lord spoke to me out of Luke 9:23. "Whoever desires to come after me let him deny 'his' self." I saw the words in a little vision. "Let him deny his self-" with a hyphen after self. The first word I saw after the hyphen was–"sufficiency." Deny your self–sufficiency. Deny your self–reliance. Deny your self–gratification. Deny your self–promotion. Deny your self–consciousness. (I believe that God wants a holy unselfconsciousness around our life. When Moses came down from the mountain, his face was shining and he didn't know it. They had to tell him.) Deny your self–centeredness. Deny your self–absorption. Deny your self–assurance. (It's different than confidence in God. It's phony confidence. It's blowing up pretend muscles under your shirt, and then the Holy Spirit has to come along with the ministry of the pin.) Deny your self–congratulation. Deny your self–satisfaction. Deny your self–willedness. (That means that you have an unsanctified tenaciousness about you that's unyielding). Deny your self–serving. Deny your self–seeking. Deny your self-made religion. Deny the hyphenated sins.

Human beings are weak, desperately weak. We must tell human beings how weak they are. We will not behold the Lord unless we are in touch with our weakness. Second Corinthians tells about the power of God that is perfected in the context of admitting human weakness and then allowing that human weakness to be translated into a dynamic interactive relationship with the kingdom of God. Our weakness is displaced with God's strength, not in a one-time experience but in a rhythm of death and resurrection. Like the action of an ocean wave sometimes it's death, sometimes it's resurrection.

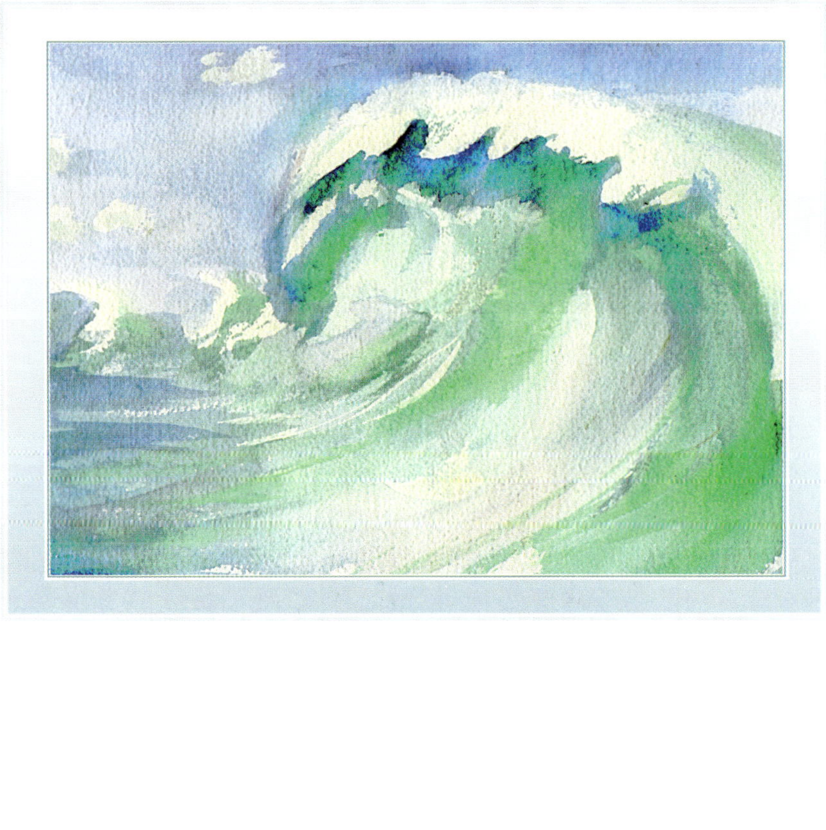

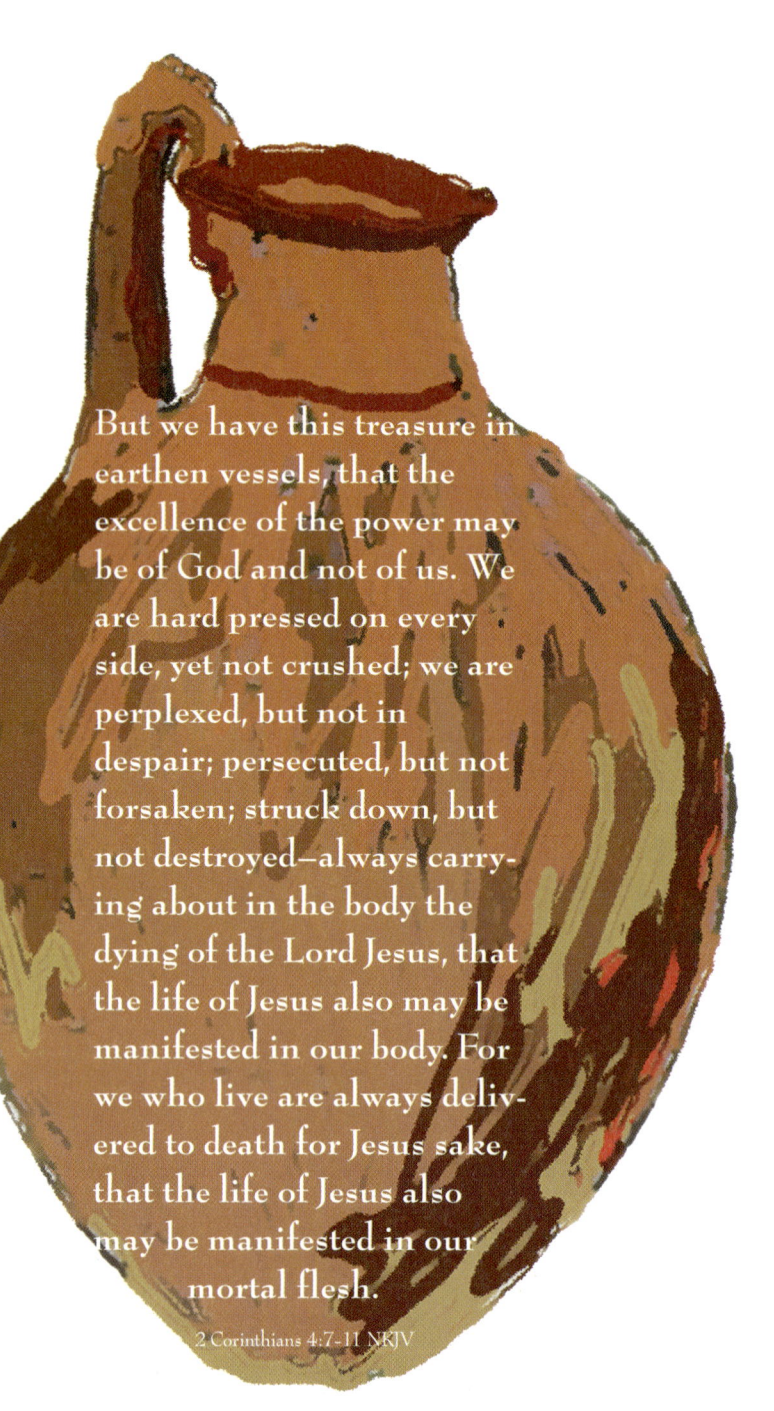

But we have this treasure in earthen vessels, that the excellence of the power may be of God and not of us. We are hard pressed on every side, yet not crushed; we are perplexed, but not in despair; persecuted, but not forsaken; struck down, but not destroyed—always carrying about in the body the dying of the Lord Jesus, that the life of Jesus also may be manifested in our body. For we who live are always delivered to death for Jesus sake, that the life of Jesus also may be manifested in our mortal flesh.

2 Corinthians 4:7-11 NKJV

Our Father,

When we hear Your Word, it stirs something strange within us—a longing for more, a longing for something deeper, a longing for an interface with the powers of the age to come. Father, we are weak in ourselves and we are not ashamed to say so because You're the one who declared all flesh is grass. Lord, our flesh profits us nothing unless it is subordinated to Your Holy Spirit. And so we ask now that You would give us the courage to face our weaknesses, to admit them, not to deny them, and to bring the brokenness of our weakness to You, Lord. You have put the treasure in an earthen vessel, and we are the earthen vessel. Allow us to be seen as weak, Lord. We're too wrapped up in our image. We're spinning our energies, managing our image. Forgive us Lord.

Lord, I feel these pressures. I feel these temptations so often. I pray that You would burn into me a resolution not to do this in my life, my relationships, and my ministry. Give us all Your attitude toward self. Show us, Lord, where we differ from You and help us as we're facing the upcoming divine disruption of the earth and of our own comfort zones. Lord, we pray that You would help us. Help us face our fears. Lift us up above our fears. Help us to face our self sins, our hyphenated sins. Help us to take them to the cross, and then bring us forth in resurrection life that we might know You, the power of Your resurrection and the fellowship of Your sufferings. Lord let that secret life that motivated the Apostle Paul motivate us as well.

FOLLOW THE LAMB

Deep unto Gethsemane's night
We follow suffering life in You
While the wine press collects light
From the fruit of love, pain grew.

Wide unto outlying lands
We travel after Abraham
Going where the Lord commands
Following the suffering Lamb.

High unto the Lamb filled throne
We climb past bounds of death to light
The Lamb's surrounded by His own
Robed in blood washed holy white.

> These are they
> who have come out of
> the great tribulation;
> they have washed
> their robes and
> made them white
> in the blood
> of the Lamb.
> Revelation 7:14

SHALL I BE THERE?

Someone who envies me
Who's scratched and stung and slapped
And sent me away is sick today.
She's sick in body and sick in soul.
My enemy is weak
and desperately needs care.
Shall I be there?

Should I wait for another word
When I've already heard—
"Don't turn away your kin."
"I've died for every person."
"Do good to those who hurt you."
"Lukewarm love is sin."

Gethsemane's night,
Love's wrestling within Christ,
Has lit a way.
Help me to follow the Lamb.

Moravian Lamb

Help me to sing—
I will follow.
I will follow, follow the Lamb.
Wherever love leads me, I'll follow.
I'll follow, I'll follow the Lamb.

Yes Lord, I will follow.
I will follow, follow the Lamb.
Give me the courage to follow.
I'll follow, I'll follow the Lamb.

Yes Lord, I will follow.
I will follow, follow the Lamb.
Whatever it costs, I will follow.
I'll follow, I'll follow the Lamb.

The Chorus *Follow the Lamb* is not original; the author is unknown. These stanza variations are new.

MORE THAN LIFE

Genesis 22

Lori Hall

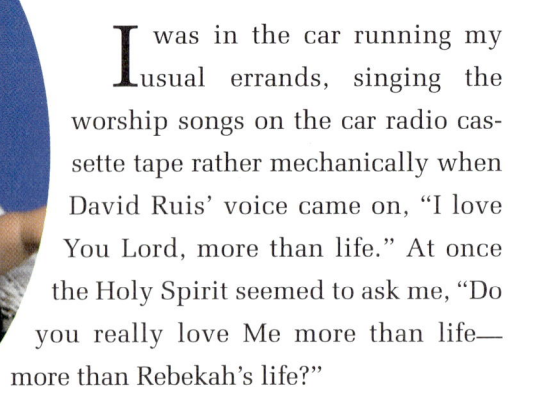

I was in the car running my usual errands, singing the worship songs on the car radio cassette tape rather mechanically when David Ruis' voice came on, "I love You Lord, more than life." At once the Holy Spirit seemed to ask me, "Do you really love Me more than life—more than Rebekah's life?"

Rebekah, our second child, has been on God's altar since birth. You see, Rebekah has hydrocephalus, a condition where the spinal fluid doesn't drain out of the brain. When she was three days old, she had an operation to install a shunt to drain the excess spinal fluid. The doctors concluded that her drainage aqueduct was blocked by a brain tumor.

Since the growth is on the brain stem, they will not consider operating unless it grows and causes additional problems. Right now, at four months old, her health is stable, but they may have to monitor her with tests the rest of her life.

"Do you really love Me—more than Rebekah's life?" The question took me off guard, and I began to think of all the possibilities we could face—chemotherapy, radiation treatments, multiple operations, and endless tests—all on my little girl. I remembered the little boy I saw a few days before in the grocery store. He was obviously going through some type of chemo or radiation. He looked about eight years old, very pale, thin, and mostly bald. I remember in tears silently praying, "Give that family strength, and please Lord, may this not be the cup we are to drink."

My thoughts drifted back to the first five years of our marriage when I longed to have children. I cried out to God for a taste of motherhood. Oh, how I could relate to Hannah! Finally, I asked God to remove the desire to have children from my heart or to grant it. I couldn't bear living in between any longer. Then, at that point, it happened! A month later I found out I was pregnant with our first child, Nathan. After that, I knew each child God would give us was truly a gift to be used ultimately for His purposes and glory. Just as Hannah gave Samuel to the Lord, we too, would give each child to the Lord. Up to this point, this was all theory—just words with good intentions. Now, however, it seemed God was asking me to physically, emotionally, and spiritually lay Rebekah's life on the altar.

"Why not my life, God?" Certainly I could negotiate my way out of this question. God knew I would gladly take all of Rebekah's problems in a heartbeat and wear them as my own. When I gave my life to Christ, I was fully aware that He might choose to use it for His Kingdom in any way He desired. Esther sums it up with her words, "If I perish, I perish"(Esther 4:16).

Laying one's own life down is one thing, laying the life of your child on the altar as Abraham did Isaac is another. It is a nice Bible story to read to our children, but walking it out is a different ball game. If, as some people say, Abraham acted in faith knowing God would provide the lamb, wasn't he still willing to sacrifice Isaac—no matter what? Wasn't it only after his knife was raised and he was fully ready to kill His son that God spoke? How willing was I to trust God? He would never ask me to sacrifice my daughter, but He was asking me to emotionally and spiritually lay her on the altar and trust Him with her life. I had prayed with hundreds of others across the world for her complete healing. What if this was not to be, would I then still trust God no matter what road we had to walk down?

As the song ended, I choked out my response with tears running down my face, "Yes Lord, I love you more than the life of my precious little girl. She is your daughter on loan to us." From his car seat, my alert two year old, Nathan, noticed my disposition change and said, "Mommy cry."

I smiled through my tears and responded, "Yes Nathan, Mommies cry too."

Rebekah is now 10 months old and after her last MRI, the neurosurgeon's exact words were, "Her growth is dissolving." By September of 1997, the MRI showed a substantial portion of the tumor had disappeared! I am ecstatic and will continue to seek God daily for complete healing of Rebekah; however, my faith does not depend on it. God is sovereign and my faith will continue to be in Him, no matter what the outcome.

Now it came to pass after these things that God tested Abraham, and said to him, "Abraham!"
And he said, "Here I am."

Then He said, "Take now your son, your only son Isaac, whom you love, and go to the land of Moriah, and offer him there as a burnt offering on one of the mountains of which I shall tell you.
And Abraham said, "My son, God will provide for Himself the lamb for a burnt offering." So the two of them went together.

Then they came to the place of which God had told him.
And Abraham built an altar there and placed the wood in order;
and he bound Isaac his son and laid him on the altar, upon the wood.
And Abraham stretched out his hand and took the knife to slay his son.
But the Angel of the LORD called to him from heaven and said,
"Abraham, Abraham!"
So he said, "Here I am."
And He said, "Do not lay your hand on the lad, or do anything to him;
for now I know that you fear God,
since you have not withheld your son, your only son, from Me."

Then Abraham lifted his eyes and looked, and there behind him was a ram caught in a thicket by its horns. So Abraham went and took the ram, and offered it up for a burnt offering instead of his son.
And Abraham called the name of the place, The-Lord-Will Provide; as it is said to this day, "In the Mount of the LORD it shall be provided."

Genesis 22:1–2; 8-13 NKJV

MY OFFERING

Rebekah is Yours
        on loan to me
On Isaac's altar
        I do place her.

I will build the altar
        as Abraham
Not in my own strength
        but by Your hand.

Though my faith is weak
        I will trust You
Rebekah,
        God has provided the Lamb.

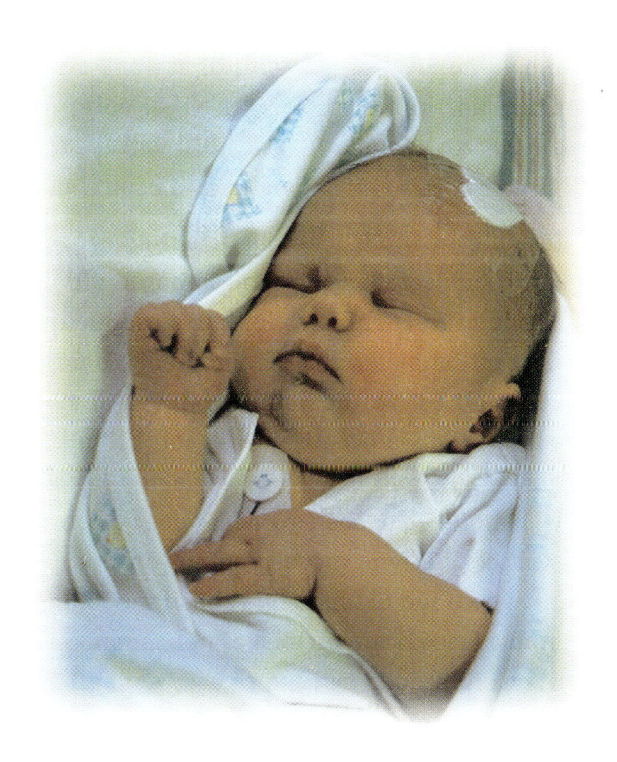

GIVER OF LIFE

For the blood that You have shed
      For the welcome mat You've spread
           At the cross

To the redeeming cross of tears
      That has shattered death and fears
           Jesus we come

For this communion sweet
      We gather at Your feet
           Giver of Life.

I have given them the glory you gave me, so that they may be one, as we are—I in them and you in me, all being perfected into one. Then the world will know that you sent me and will understand that you love them as much as you love me.

      John 17:22-23

WHAT CAN I OFFER

O what can I offer to the King of Kings
And what can be brought for
The One who owns all things?
Now here on the altar is the gift I bring
From my heart through Your Spirit to You.

Lord and Savior, my Healer and my King,
Sovereign Maker, I owe You everything.
Have Your way Lord, my all to You I bring.

> And I lay it before You
> Here at Your feet,
> My life here before You
> To use as You please.

O what can I offer—
every breath I breathe,
The minutes and hours
that You have given me?

> So Spirit of power
> Fall afresh on me,
> Fill my heart and my soul.
> You've kindled a fire
> Let it rise to the King.

HIS JOY

We are familiar with Jesus as the tortured and martyred Son of God, but can we conceive of Him as laughing, dancing, singing, and having fun? Even John the Baptist jumped for joy inside his mother's womb when he first met Jesus, who was still within Mary. At Jesus' birth, the angels declared to the shepherds, "I bring you good news of GREAT JOY for everyone!" (Luke 2:10 NLT). In response, they hurried to find Him for themselves.

Joy heralded His beginning as a son of man and faithfully traveled with Him every day on earth. Within the person of Jesus are wellsprings of joy that have no end. He even endured the cross for the JOY held before Him. Yes, He was able to go through great pain and agony because of the love that He had for His Father—but that perfect love is full of an unspeakable joy that is glorious!

Everywhere Jesus walked, the new wine of joy and love spilled out upon mankind's heartaches and pains, healing the sick, raising the dead, delivering men from demons, and setting captives free. Is it any wonder that we are still irresistibly drawn to the joy-filled fountain of His abundant life?

While Jesus was still a baby, Simeon prophesied that He would be rejected by many, and that it would be their undoing. Yet for many others, He would be their greatest joy (Luke 2:34 NLT)! We will never find lasting joy without knowing Jesus; however, sometimes His joy will be misunderstood or rejected.

Let us come to Him as little children and find the joy of Jesus!

OUR JOY

Dear brothers and sisters,

Whenever trouble comes your way, let it be an opportunity for joy. For when your faith is tested, your endurance has a chance to grow. So let it grow, for when your endurance is fully developed, you will be strong in character and ready for anything.   James 1:2-4 NLT

How can we think of hard places as opportunities for joy to flourish? From James' viewpoint, if we cooperate with the creative work of the cross in times of crisis, our own desires will die and the Lord's desires will live. As His character is fully developed in us, we will be steadfast in the storms. Our anchor will hold because we will be fastened deeply within the rock of His character.

Although God does not cause all of our troubles, He does allow them. Yet He never leaves us or forsakes us, and He remains close at every turn of events. As we turn to Him in troubles, He increases our love for Him and builds our faith in His love for us. When we are too strong in ourselves, we cannot lean on Him and find our true strength in the joy of the Lord.

Sometimes He even designs our trials to bring freedom to those who are watching us. If we can be like Paul and Silas and keep our gaze steadily focused upon Him in the midst of our painful "beatings," every prison door can fly open and every restrictive chain can fall off as Jesus' joy comes to set the captives free.

His heart is sure; His hands are larger and stronger than our own. Only He can steady our souls in the midst of distress. He brings forth good in every situation for those who love Him and are called according to His purposes. Jesus is the center of our joy!

LIFE MUST GO ON *Kayla Apon, age 8*

God knows your problems, God hears your cries
And He wants to tell you things are all right
Everything is our Master's design
Sometimes in life He must weave a black line.

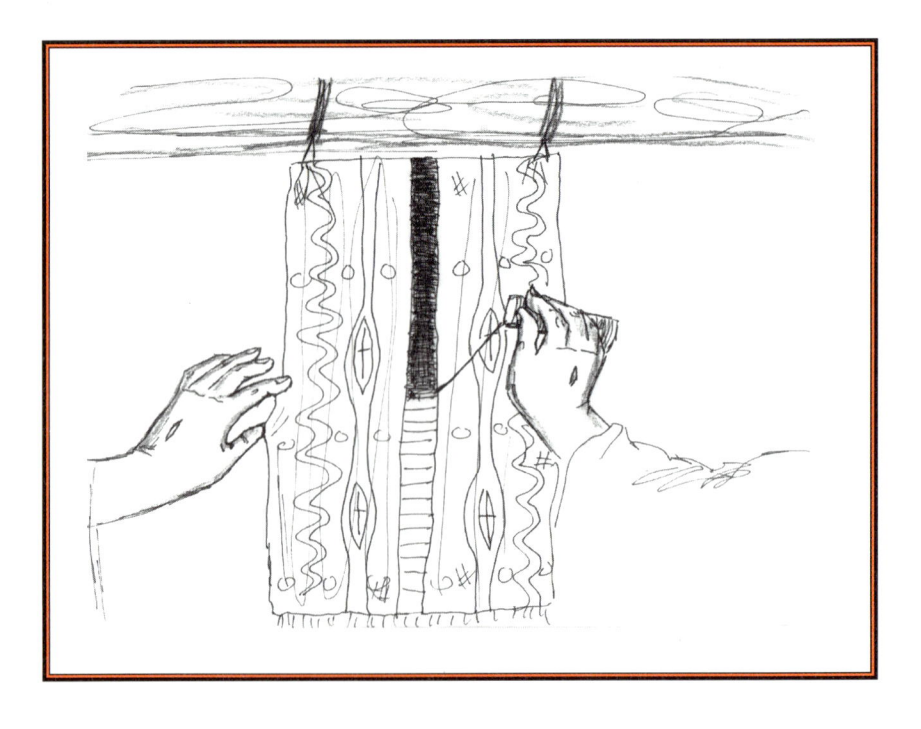

Abigail Apon, age 10

IMMORTALITY

Exalting pain was not God's plan
When He showed man immortality.
He simply killed the "death" in death
To end the lie of its fatality.

SIGNIFICANT SACRIFICE

Oh Lord, give me an understanding of what You did on the cross.
Let it be so real that I feel as though
I am standing there amidst the curious,
hostile onlookers at Calvary.
    Seeing Your violated body
        Hearing the cry of Your last words,
            Reading the accusation above Your head:
                "King of the Jews."

Lord, give me an appreciation of the depths of Your darkness
With a glimpse of the glory of Your light.
Let Your holiness be so real that I feel as though
I am there to witness the aftermath of Your death.
    Seeing the darkness over the land
        Hearing the splitting of rocks
            and the tearing of the curtain in the Temple
            and the centurion's realization:
                "Surely this was the Son of God."

Lord, give me the revelation of Your death's significance for me.
Let Your sacrifice be so real that I feel as though
I am sitting in the courtroom
waiting to receive the penalty of death
for a crime I have committed.
    Seeing You take my seat
    Gesturing for me to walk out the door into freedom.
    Hearing the gavel fall,
        and the judge's words declaring me righteous and clean
            but You, guilty and sentenced to death
                for the crime you did not commit.

Lord give me a sense of Your compassion
and a desire to follow.
Let Your example be so real that I **am**
willing to suffer and to forgive,
    sacrificing my time and energy in
        caring for Your sheep.

Lord give me a heartfelt knowledge
of Your unceasing, perfect love
both at the cross on Calvary
and in my daily life.

Let Your heart be so real that I know You are with me
Seeing my hardened heart and the damage it has done,
    Hearing my every secret thought and word, yet
        Yearning for fellowship with me and
            Considering me a gift from the Father.

You came from Your throne in heaven
to suffer and die
so that I might live
in peace and in paradise.

Angel with one of the ten virgins
Used by permission.

Now this is eternal life, that they may know You,
the only true God, and Jesus Christ, whom You have sent. John 17:3 NKJV

CHOOSE

Perhaps the greatest pain we know
Is when the tears no longer flow
When disillusionment is high
And voiceless throats gape to the sky.

For silence digs into the bone
When all our passion borne alone
Spreads like a sickness to the joints
And full of pain, to life we point.

With every gesture full of rage
But in our words we soft engage,
Lest men may see who helped to scar
And add to those we bear so far.

Yet here in hands of mortal men
Our Father oft' begins again
By binding up the wounds of youth
With words of empathy and truth.

And we must choose, on mortal's side
To be a patient, truthful guide.
As those one helps must also choose
The yokes of bondage then to lose.

What is the human face of God.

the strangulated Christ vulnerable to taunts

suffering servants will change the world.

Cry the Gospel — it's the only way to live

Stand fast beside Him My identity depends on it

ALTARS

Just the other day
I sensed God asking me to pray
For a someone who seemed quite confident
And sure about their way—
A someone who'd hurt my feelings,
Shamed me before my friends,
Talked behind my back,
Usurped my place,
And refused to bend.

The church was almost empty.
She sat apart, almost alone
Facing the big cross banner
Like a scowling judgment stone.

At first my ear was hard,
My heart was cold
Nothing in me could do
What He asked me to.

Running from rejection,
Turning from her need,
I did a foolish thing.
Right there, with all the prayer group looking
I climbed up on a higher chair
And put my hand, smack dab, right where
His heart had bled on the cross.

I got a little dizzy
Half afraid that I might fall
And seem a fool,
Balancing there so long—
My hand hugging the banner
On the empty church wall,
Pulling the love down so literally
From that cross into me.

But it worked.
Soon there was no hurt,
Only love. Such love.

A SONG

Lord You invite us to join You
At the feast You have prepared for us.
We are to make ourselves ready
So we will be called unto You.

Chorus: How wonderful it will be
To feast at the table You have prepared.
You will be there eating with us.
What a glorious honor!

What a glorious honor
To be sitting next to our King
Talking about the things of heaven,
Filled with awe at His majesty and power
His humbleness and merciful nature.

All I ever wanted was to see You.
But now I am seated at Your table
Feasting with You,
Feasting with You!

Tirana, Albania 1996

Here I am! I stand at the door and knock.
If anyone hears my voice and opens the door,
I will come in and eat with him, and he with me.

Revelation 3:20

COMMUNION

I give my life to You.
You gave Your life for mine.
Covenant cup upon a tree.
Your blood for me.

Blood mingled
In communion wine
Eternal life
poured into time
Mine is Yours
And Yours is mine.

THE GOODNESS OF GOD

Have you tasted and seen the Goodness of God?

Won't you come, take of the water without price
Which has poured from His side,
That you would thirst no more?

Have you eaten His bread,
The life given in the flesh for you,
The incredible Body of God
That you would hunger no more, only for Him?

Have you looked on His face,
His passion given for joy
That you may be saved?

Have you touched His hands
Wounded for love
That you might be His?

Have you tasted and seen
the Goodness of God?

> For the LORD is good;
> His mercy is everlasting,
> And His truth *endures*
> to all generations.
> Psalm 100:5 NKJV

© Used with permission.

For I received from the Lord what I also passed on to you:
The Lord Jesus, on the night he was betrayed, took bread,
and when he had given thanks, he broke it and said,
"This is my body, which is for you; do this in remembrance of me."
In the same way, after supper he took the cup, saying,
"This cup is the new covenant in my blood;
do this, whenever you drink it, in remembrance of me."
For whenever you eat this bread and drink this cup,
you proclaim the Lord's death until he comes.

Therefore, whoever eats the bread or drinks the cup of the Lord in an unworthy manner will be guilty of sinning against the body and blood of the Lord. A man ought to examine himself before he eats of the bread and drinks of the cup. For anyone who eats and drinks without recognizing the body of the Lord eats and drinks judgment on himself.

1 Cor. 11:23-29

As we eat communion bread and drink of the communion cup, as we remember Him and proclaim His death, let us enter into true communion with Him and with one another.

PARTAKING UNWORTHILY: A COMMUNION SERMON

Ben Binckley

Have you ever felt hesitant to take communion? Some Christians refuse to take communion for fear of doing so "unworthily" and bringing judgment upon themselves. Others take communion regularly, but have vague fears of doing so in an unworthy manner and bringing condemnation upon themselves rather than receiving the healing grace of God. Many Christians are confused by St. Paul's statement, "Whoever eats the bread or drinks the cup of the Lord in an unworthy manner will be guilty of profaning the body and blood of the Lord (1 Cor. 11:27 NASB).

St. Paul did not refer to universal unworthiness when he wrote of partaking unworthily. We are all unworthy of God's great love and of Christ's sacrifice. In the sacrament, as in life, we trust and depend for our salvation upon the mercy of God who loves us though unworthy, and who, while we were yet sinners sent His only Son to suffer death upon the Cross to redeem our ungodly souls. Eating the bread or drinking the cup in an "unworthy manner," refers to the spirit in which we commune not to being undeserving.

First, we cannot commune with Christ with a factious and dividing spirit. St. Paul refers to divisions and factions among church members (1 Cor.11:18). Social and class distinctions, cliques, *any* partitions which divide rather than unite the body of Christ witness against the devotion of Christians to their Heavenly Father. God wants all races, ages, economic, and social levels united in one holy fellowship of love for His Son, devoted to each other and all men. Every dividing wall of hostility between men will be broken down by the love of God in Christ. Christ awaits only the willingness of each of us to let His love fill our hearts and His Spirit rule our lives. Thus, those who seek to create and perpetuate division in the church grieve the Holy Spirit, partake unworthily of the communion sacrament, and miss true communion with Christ.

Second, we cannot commune with Christ with an unforgiving spirit. When we pray the Lord's Prayer, we ask our heavenly Father to "forgive us our trespasses as we forgive those who trespass against us." It is easy to say the words, but difficult to live them. Is there anyone who has trespassed against you, wronged you, or embarrassed you against whom you are treasuring hard feelings in your heart? Forgive that person! You can do so, completely—from the bottom of your heart. Simply recollect *your* offenses against God and remember that at your asking and through your faith in Christ, He forgives you completely. Forgiveness is essential to the restoration of any broken relationship. If we do not forgive those who offend us, God will not forgive us. Christ only communes with those who approach His table with a forgiving spirit.

Third, we cannot commune with Christ with an unrepentant spirit. Jesus said, "If you are offering your gift at the altar and there remember that your brother has something against you, leave your gift there before the altar and go: first be reconciled to your brother and then come and offer your gift" (Matt 5:23-24). If you know your brother has "something against you," or if you know you have sinned against another, the repentant spirit goes to the other and asks forgiveness for any trespass. Forgiving and repenting before taking Holy Communion is needed if Communion is to transcend ritual and become a true meeting with Christ.

Fourth, we cannot commune with Christ with an irreverent spirit. St. Paul describes irreverence as follows: "When you meet together it is not the Lord's Supper that you eat. For in eating, each one goes ahead with his own meal, and one is hungry and another drunk" (v. 21). Apparently there were some gluttonous and irreverent souls in the church at Corinth who took the Lord's Supper, not in remembrance of what Christ had done, but to fill their stomachs or get drunk. Treating Holy things in an unholy way is blasphemy or sacrilege. It will bring judgment. Paul said contempt for what is to be respected as sacred is "profaning the body and blood of the Lord."

Today we do not take communion to make up for a lost meal, but some of us do take the Lord's Supper lightly or with a matter-of-fact heart, thinking that communion is not important. This inwardly encourages cynicism and scoffing at the Lord, His Body the Church, and His means of grace. This is to partake unworthily and reject an opportunity for communion with Him.

Father,

> *Forgive us if we have over taken Holy Communion in an unworthy manner: with a divisive spirit, an unforgiving spirit, an unrepentant spirit, or an irreverent spirit. Deliver us all from bringing judgment upon ourselves through unworthy participation in Your Holy Sacrament. Bring us into true Communion with You and with Your Son.*

A HIDDEN PLACE

Hidden deep within my heart
Safe from doubt and injury
There's a place I cannot enter
Carelessly.

A burning place of brilliant Light
Filled with Harmony
It's a place I never enter
Unless love beckons me.

A place aflame with molten love,
Soaked with Majesty,
This place is only entered
With humility.

If Cherubim with flaming sword
Would guard the door from me
The place is entered by Christ's blood
Most confidently.

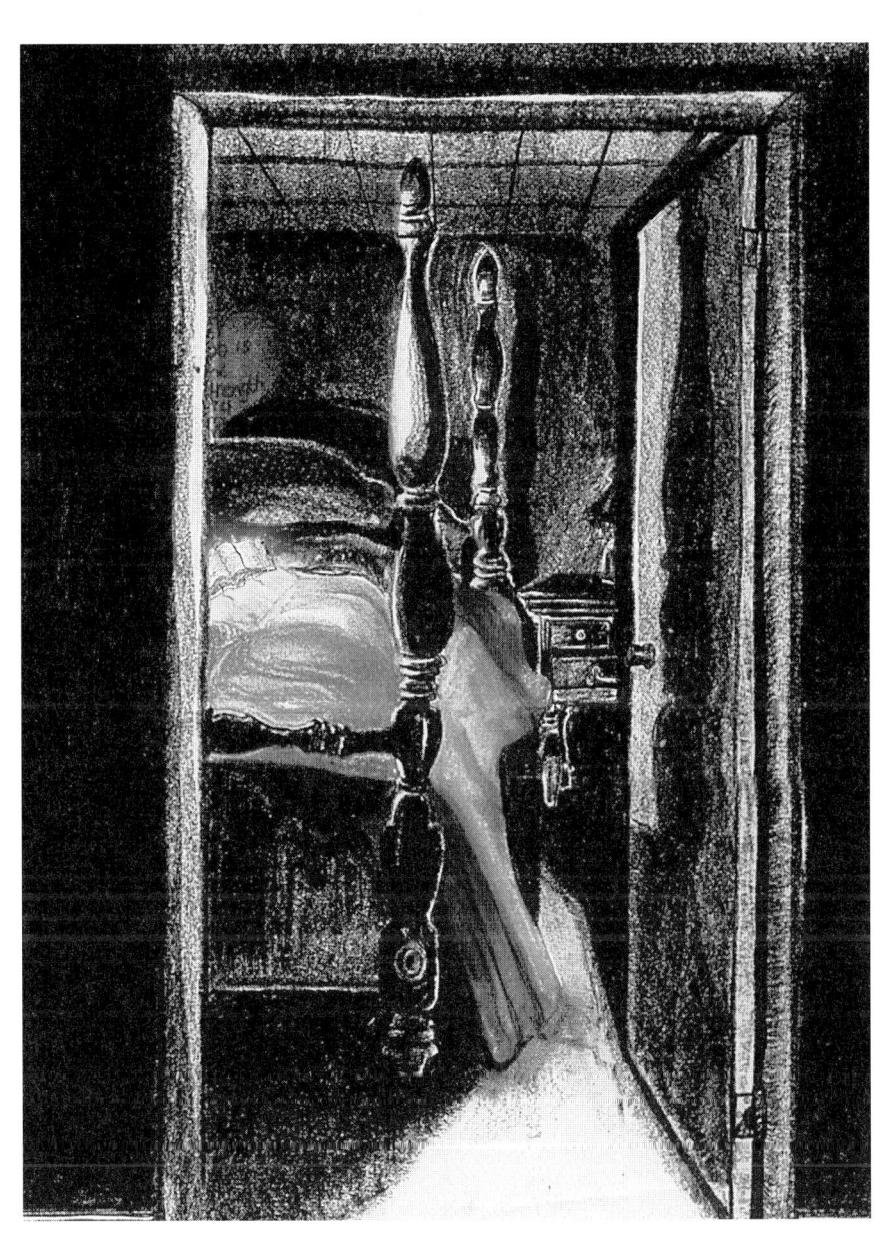

But you, when you pray, go into your inner room,
and when you have shut your door,
pray to your Father who is in secret,
and your Father who sees in secret will repay you.

Matthew 6:6 NASB

ALL I CAN DO — A SONG

O Lord, how can I forget
That on the cross You paid the price—for me.
I recall the day You called my name
And how it felt to be set free!
Jesus, why would you want me,
A sinner and a stranger to Your ways?
To think that I am in the Master's plan
Since time began
For eternity.

Chorus:
And all I can do is bow before You
No words can tell how great You are.
All I can do is fall before You.
I love You.
I love You.

O Lord, give us power to grasp
The wonder and the greatness of Your love.
Creator God, it fills our hearts with awe
That we are Yours, consuming fire!
Jesus, Holy Lamb of God
How beautiful the bright and Morning Star.
You love to be where all Your children sing
And worship bring. . . .
So here You are.

Repeat Chorus

CLASPED HANDS

As members of the body, Christ
With entwined hearts we do unite
To circle 'bout His throne in dance
His love is shared through hands which clasp.

For two are better than the one
Where strength is left when day is done
And surely multiplied must be
The power in community.

Where men in need are not reviled
But helped through each and every trial
Where rivalry is fast replaced
By weeping, humble hands of grace.

For here in bonds of unity
The man accepted will be freed
To cast off weights and take up arms
His spirit for the battle warmed.

Encouraged as he runs his race
The prayers of others set His pace
One day before the Lord we'll stand
To praise our King—with claspéd hands.

DILIGENCE

I have longed to worship You
> without the masks I've full removed.
When I've laid them down at last
> with my expectations past
No more to be fooled by me
> or the things men wish to see
Gently hearing with my heart
> all the truth You shall impart.
Here I'll put the roles behind
> finding You my only guide
With no drama, nor pretense
> only quiet diligence.

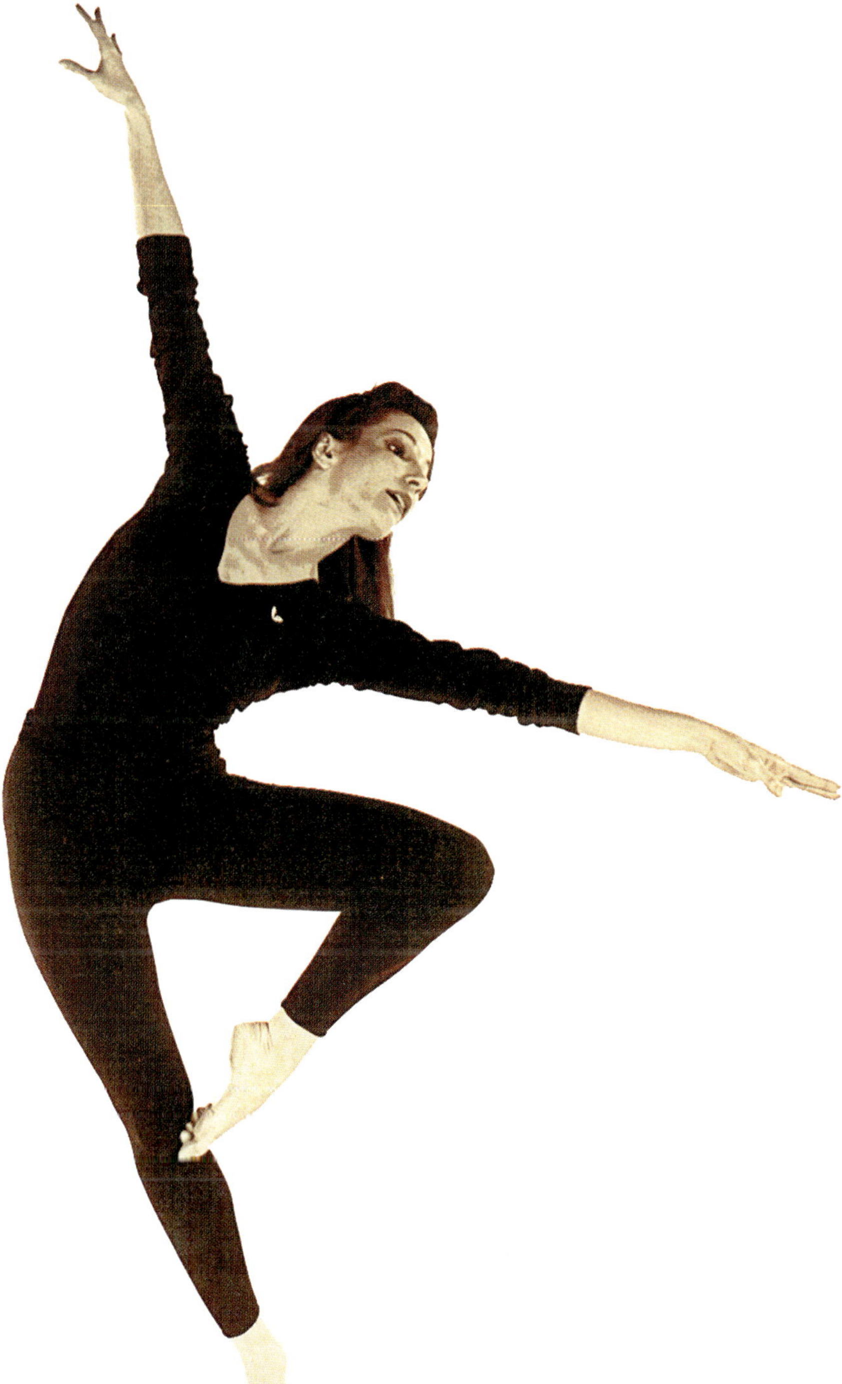

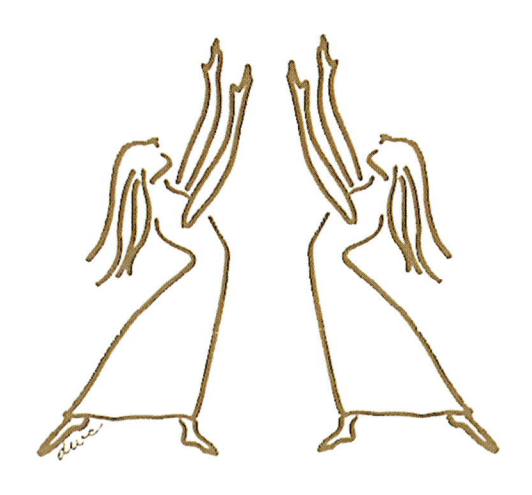

WORSHIPPING INTO THE HEART OF GOD
Diane Wawrejko Cochran, ©Dances Wawrejko. Used by permission.

As a performing artist, I am excited and blessed with the artistry of God in the Old Testament metaphors which foreshadow salvation through Jesus. I am particularly touched by the metaphors and symbols God has given us to teach us how to enter into intimate worship with Him. In Psalm 100:4, God commands us to

> Enter His gates with Thanksgiving and His courts with praise;
> give thanks to Him and praise His name.

When it was written, this verse referred to entering the actual physical temple, the courtyard and building. Entering into the temple is a metaphor for our spiritual worship.

The picture begins about 3,000 years ago in Exodus 36-40 when Moses describes God's design for a portable temple (called a tabernacle) to be built in the wilderness—a temple that could be constructed, struck (a theater term for tearing down a set), and transported during the Israelites' 40 years of wandering in the desert. This portable temple was the only temple of worship sanctioned by God until Solomon built the temple in Jerusalem in 966 B.C. The Jerusalem temple was built on Mt. Moriah, where Abraham had built an altar to sacrifice Isaac, the son promised to him by God (2 Chron. 3–4). At the time of King David, Mt Moriah was the threshing floor, the place where the grain is separated from the chaff, of the barn of Araunah the Jebusite. David purchased the land from Araunah for the Temple.

All the colors, patterns, garments, furnishings, etc. of the temple picture spiritual truth. The architectural design is one picture of our present spiritual worship. With your visual imagination, picture a building. The building is the house of worship. This house of worship is surrounded completely by an outer court; the outer court is surrounded completely by a wall with 12 gates. This entire structure is "the temple."

To enter into worship, the people passed through the gates and into the courts. Psalm 100 teaches us to enter worship with thanksgiving and praise. Worship is a joyous occasion! Inside the courtyard was an altar and a laver or huge bronze basin for washing. The basin is a picture of Christ cleansing our souls from the filth of sin so that we can come near to a Holy God. The altar of burnt offering was positioned in front of the entrance to the tabernacle. After making the blood sacrifice at the altar for the atonement for sins, the worshipper could enter into the tabernacle (house) of God. What a beautiful metaphor for the sacrifice Jesus made on the cross for us! He was the sacrificial lamb whose blood was shed for the forgiveness of sins. Once we accept the blood sacrifice made for us, we are permitted to enter into fellowship with God (tabernacle). In both the tabernacle in the wilderness and the Jerusalem temples, God's presence was manifested by thick clouds inside the tabernacle.

Inside the tabernacle was a table of shewbread (representing our fellowship with Jesus and one another), a lampstand (the Holy Spirit), and the altar of incense (the prayers and worship of believers). Behind these, the curtain to the Holy of Holies hid the ark of the covenant containing the Mosaic tablets on which were written the Ten Commandments.

The curtain and the Holy of Holies are very significant. Only the High Priest was allowed to go behind the curtain and then only once a year after following a prescribed ritual of bathing to signify His desire for purity. On the Day of Atonement he could enter the Holy of Holies and meet face-to-face with the Creator of the universe to intercede for the sins of the nation of Israel! The High Priest was the *only* person with this privilege. When Jesus breathed His last breath on the cross, the curtain in the temple was rent in two from top to bottom (Matt. 27:51).

What does this mean for us? It means that the blood of Jesus, as both our sacrificial lamb and our High Priest, opened the way for us to freely have access to the heart of God! We no longer need a human mediator to go behind the curtain and intercede for us; Jesus is the only mediator between God and man (1 Tim. 2:5).

Do we *fully* enter into worship? Many Christians stay in the outer courts and are content with merely giving thanksgiving and praise. To enter more deeply into God's heart, to experience deep fellowship with Him, we must confess *all* our sins. We must wait upon Him and earnestly seek His presence. How many of us are willing to be still and wait for the thick cloud of the Lord's presence to envelop us? How many of us are willing to enter behind the Holy of Holies and experience face-to-face communion with the Lord of all? It's not easy. It takes a life of discipline and holiness, a heart of purity that seeks God for Himself alone. What a privilege to enter into God's heart and allow the Maker of the universe to speak with us!

Therefore, brethren, having boldness to enter the Holiest by the blood of Jesus, by a new and living way which He consecrated for us, through the veil, that is, His flesh, and having a High Priest over the house of God, let us draw near with a true heart in full assurance of faith, having our hearts sprinkled from an evil conscience and our bodies washed with pure water.   Hebrews 10:19-22 NKJV

MIRROR OF LOVE

You stooped to earth
to hang on the cross
Arms raised to the Father
Open to embrace humanity
As it slay you.

Mouth and Hands of the Creator
Showing us the Father
Man has touched, seen and heard God
because You came.

You know the Father best
You've sat beside Him
and walked and talked with Him
in a way we have never known
And yet You left His side
to fulfill His will
And complete His plan with a love and trust so strong
that You uncompromisingly took the cup.

Way to the Father
Link to the God we've feared
Reconciling us to Him
Revealing His love for us
Praise You, Lord Jesus
for becoming one of us
and then returning to the glory
You possessed before the world began.

Where can I go from Your Spirit?
Or where can I flee from Your presence?
If I ascend into the heaven, You *are* there;
If I make my bed in hell, behold, You are there.
If I take the wings of the morning,
And dwell in the uttermost parts of the sea,
Even there Your hand shall lead me,
And Your right hand shall hold me.

Psalm 139:7-10 NKJV

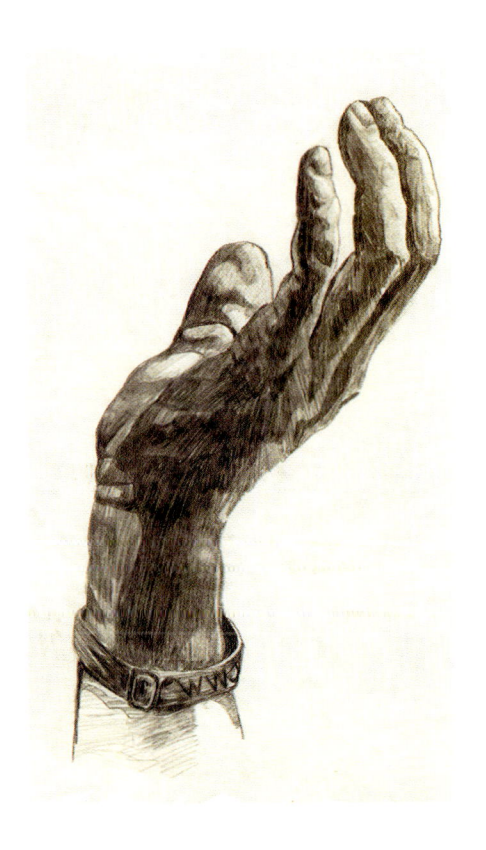

Used by permission.

"Come now, let us reason together," says the Lord.
Though your sins be as scarlet they shall be white as snow.

Isaiah 1:18

May 29, 1998

Beloved of God,

There is something within us that dreads to face ourselves, and beyond that, longs to be right, to justify and defend ourselves, more often than not at the expense of others. Jesus said that there is only one good (right) and that was God. Being Himself Almighty God, that was quite a mouthful. With that saying He forever identified with us in our humanity. He humbled Himself beyond understanding, and yet we long to be justified. For some time I have seen that even when we are right, we can be so right that we are dead wrong. That is the road to failure. The flesh will rise and all it knows is death.

There is an entering into the knowledge that apart from His presence and the constant fellowship known as prayer, we are lonely beyond bearing and have no desire to live without His sweet essence. The price to be paid is humanly unbearable because we are made to see ourselves and abhor what we see. What is the answer to this dreaded vision of our hearts? Death at any cost! No price is too great to be rid of this earth nature, the horror of this flesh life. What is the key? A bloody cross where we are impaled like our Lord and dread Sovereign.

Who is it that so cruelly hangs us there before all the world to see? The same one Who hung His only begotten Son, full of grace and truth. Jesus commanded us to take up our cross and follow Him. How euphoric that sounds, how noble and grand. The cruel act administered through the hands of saints and sinners is beyond words and carries the same shame and stigma of Calvary. He did not deserve it. We cannot say the same. And yet we strive to protect ourselves. We fulfill the flesh nature and judge others from eyes blinded by self when we need to be blinded by love that we might truly see. Oh, we may or may not say anything because we are so religious, but it is in all of our hearts to be right in our own eyes. There is our undoing. We were commanded to take up our cross. I would encourage everyone who hears this message to not just choose the cross but to cry out for its embrace and bless the One Who nails us to it. We hear our Savior say to take up your cross and follow Me. That's not too bad. We don't mind picking it up and toting it around once in a while, but when He bids us to lie down as He did and allow the Father to nail us to it that we might die—now that's another story. Whoa! Wait a minute! That can't be God! We start rebuking the devil and everyone else. "How can they have said this? How could they have done that?" We defend ourselves and justify ourselves when Christ would not defend or justify His own self. Following Him, the Lord God, is our sure victory over ourselves.

Here is the narrow gate to the Kingdom of God. Here is the joy and peace that no man takes from us. We must choose not only to pick up our cross and follow Jesus, but if we would see our resurrection, then we must of necessity do as our blessed Savior did and rejoice in spirit for the joy that is set before us. We must go to the garden of Gethsemane. He is waiting for us there. We must see God the Father as the Author of our demise, choosing the cruelest of deaths that our self nature, our righteousness, our pride, and our flesh may be destroyed. Destroyed? Yes, destroyed! Oh that I might know Him in the fellowship of His suffering and the power and glory of His resurrection. Let us follow Him with grateful hearts filled with love and thanksgiving to the One Who has allowed us to be slain on that bloody tree, thanking Him and knowing that all things work for the good of those who love Him, who are called according to His purpose. Rejoice in (and with) Him in the face of every accusation, every slander, every gossip, every grief and sorrow from the hands of those who should love and cherish us as their own. Only then can we be delivered from defending ourselves and believing that we are any better than those who have spit in our faces, beaten us half to death, and pierced our hands and feet. Here and here alone is the freedom and liberty of the saints. All of us who have ever cried out to be like our Master, there is hope. There is a way. He who the Son sets free is free indeed!

Oh, how starved we have been. Have you cried out to God to be like Jesus? Here is a key! Have you longed for the blessed fruit of the Holy Spirit? Here is your key! Our resurrection will be into a deeper depth of love, joy, peace, patience, kindness, goodness, faithfulness, gentleness and self control. Do you abhor your flesh and the ugliness of the judgments and foolishness, the lack of love that has permeated your being? Here is your key! Do not turn your back on nor despair of yourself. Truly glory in the cross, the God Who gave it and the vessels that He moved through to hang you on it. He will bring you to this deeper death for which you have longed. Take no offense, but instead give it to Christ. Ask! Receive from Him the liberty of forgiveness Himself, not only for the crucifier but for ourselves. Think on this, do you need to forgive God and to ask for His forgiveness? You know the answer. If we allow it to, this setting of our faces like flint and going through crucifixion will reveal and drive out the darkness from our souls by the very light of His joy over us. If we do not allow this work, then we will merely become bitter—spending our lives crying over how we have been wronged—defending and justifying ourselves while judging others and wanting them judged by God. We become part of the problem instead of part of the answer. Have you chosen the cross only to lay it down to rehearse the wrong? Go to Gethsemane! There you can hand the Father the nails (hurts) needed to hang you to the cross. There you will receive the grace for crucifixion. There you will be assured that He will not leave you on the cross forever. Once firmly affixed to the cross, you are helpless. The Father put you there by the hands of man and the Father will remove you once you are dead to the offense. He will then be free to usher you into the resurrection of the fruit of His nature.

We love the Blood of Jesus because of the life that is in it. A price beyond speaking is what it cost. Ask for grace to pay the price of Gethsemane and the ensuing crucifixion that we have been honored with, knowing that your life and all that pertains to it is hidden with Christ in God. Embrace them and see that it comes from the hands of a loving God. Ask for grace to love the instruments of your crucifixion, and see that He is the author of it—that is where the Blood will flow. Let our hearts be full of gratitude to the living God for He desires His nature and the precious fruit of the Dove to be worked into us. Thank God Who has made a way for us to see past ourselves and into His divine plan! Rejoice! Rejoice! Rejoice! Your God has undertaken for you and has made the way where there was no way. It has never been what we have thought. It is not our works. It is not the gifts. Stand and declare! Give glory to God and thanksgiving that the Author and Finisher of our faith has been the Author and Finisher of us! There is your life hidden with God in Christ Jesus. Paul understood these things. That is why he sat in a prison at midnight worshipping the God Who had orchestrated what appeared to be his demise, his situation. That is why he was chosen to write First Corinthians, the thirteenth chapter. The prison walls were shaken and his bondage broken. Ours will be also! Rejoice evermore and again I say rejoice!

This is a hard thing of great value. Let us rise in gratitude to our Pattern who despised the cross and its shame but saw beyond it to the glory set before Him.

> Therefore Jesus also, that He might sanctify the people
> through His own blood, suffered outside the gate.
> Hence, let us go out to Him outside the camp,
> bearing His reproach.
> For here we do not have a lasting city,
> but we are seeking the city which is to come.
> Through Him then, let us continually
> offer up a sacrifice of praise to God,
> that is, the fruit of lips that give thanks to His name.
>
> Hebrews 13:12-15 NASB

Could this be the promise fulfilled in Revelation 3:7-12? Our great **Overcomer** is within us and before us, bringing resurrection if we meet with Him in the garden and let Him take us through to Life. This deep work of the Father will bring forth the nature of the Lamb. I would ask you—how and where did He accomplish this incredible deed? Was it at the crucifixion or was it at Gethsemane? Have we already been crucified and behaved badly? As long as there is breath, there is hope. Go back to the garden—He awaits us there. His mercy endures forever. His love has overwhelmed our failures for they are in multitude. As long as we say, "Yes, I know, but!" we have lost before we have started. Behold Him. Follow Him. Rejoice with Him. We will taste the fruit of His Spirit. We will rejoice in His resurrection and in ours.

These things I have spoken unto you that in Me you might have peace.
In the world you shall have tribulation; but be of good cheer
for I have overcome the world.

John 16:33 NKJV

AFTERWORD

After Jesus' resurrection, He appeared to His disciples. One of them, Thomas, was absent. Upon hearing the disciples' report of Jesus' appearance, Thomas responded, "Unless I see in His hand the print of the nails, and put my finger into the print of the nails, and put my hand into His side, I will not believe" (John 20:5 NKJV). Jesus gave Thomas that opportunity but told him, "Blessed are those who have not seen and yet have believed" (v. 29).

We can still see the crucified and glorified Jesus through the eyes of faith. Do you desire to give your life to Christ? If so, tell Him that you want to enter into newness of life with Him. His Cross has made a way for you to enter into the joy of His salvation. "I am He who lives, and was dead, and behold, I am alive forevermore. Amen. And I have the keys of Hades and of Death" (Rev. 1:18 NKJV).

If you want to ask Jesus into your heart, you can pray like this:

> *Lord Jesus, I want Your life to live in me. I want Your Spirit in my heart. Please forgive me for everything in me that falls short of Your Holiness. Lord, I give my life to You. Please give Your life to me.*

For those who have already come to a measure of faith in Jesus—do you have a hard time letting the truth of the cross and resurrection sink down into your heart from your head? Have you let worries, concerns, and distractions keep you from a radically powerful message that wants to cut through the darkness in your heart, your family, your neighborhood, community and church?

Cry out that your faith will be evident and operative in your life. You can pick up your cross and follow Him. You can see His face and know His will in ways that will not just be a religious routine that happens weekly, monthly or a few times a year.

Christ didn't see rich and poor, male and female, red and yellow, black or white. He saw men and women who were separated from the Father, men and women who needed His love. He laid down His life to bring us into that love. He didn't see inconvenience, pain or suffering as the only thing. He saw and experienced them, but He also saw joy in going to the cross because He lived His life totally for the Father. Through Him we can do the exact same thing.

Father,
I want to repent.
My desire is to receive and operate in the same faith
that Jesus had in You for His resurrection.
I cry out for it Lord,
so that You would be glorified and lifted up.
Jesus, may we have the faith that you had
to pick up our crosses and follow You.
I pray that we would seek Your face
and that we would know Your will and Your ways.
Protect us from the religious routines and enthusiasms
that happen on occasion.
Instead, give us life, and let it be Life, indeed.

THE CONTRIBUTORS' INDEX

Page   Writers/Artists
Cover: Janet Emery
8   Introduction,
         Ginny Emery and Joyce Long
10   Pencil Drawing, Janet Emery
11   Foreword, Thomas Severson
13   Photograph, Bill Emery
14   Photograph, Brad and Patti Weiss
15   Creation, Abigail Apon
16   His Plan, Ginny Emery
16   Photographs, Ginny Emery
18   Divine Longing, Joyce Long
21   Photograph, Ginny Emery
22   The Only Hope I Have,
         Laura Millirons
24   Oil Painting, Corey Hagberg
25   In Time, Ginny Emery
26   I'm Not Going to Cry, I'm Not
         Going to Cry!!! Lori Apon
28   Text, Ginny Emery
28   Computer Illustration, Janet Emery
29   Text, Ginny Emery
30   Prodigal's Puzzle,
         Photographs (3), Ginny Emery
31   Photograph, Ginny Emery
32   The Stairport, Joyce Long
33   Watercolor, Ginny Emery
35   Photograph, Ginny Emery
36   Watercolor, Ginny Emery
37   The Crucifixion, Ginny Emery
38   Watercolor, Ginny Emery
39   Watercolor, Unknown
40   That Day, Ginny Emery
41   Pencil Sketch, David Roy,
         courtesy of Dale Jaacks
42   His Obedience, N. J. Suire
45   Our Prayer, Ginny Emery
46   Jesus: The Christ, Ginny Emery
46   Pencil and Pastel drawing,
         Johan Vander Tol
47   Pencil and Pastel drawing,
         Johan Vander Tol
48   Watercolor and Computer drawing,
         Ginny Emery
49   "My God, My God, Why Have You
         Forsaken Me?" Ross Nelson

49   Watercolor/Computer, Ginny Emery
50   Putting All our Expectancies
         in the Blood of the Cross,
         C. S. Kellough
52   This Pain, Marcia Thomas
         Pencil Drawing, Janet Emery
53   Alone, Ginny Emery
         Photograph, Ginny Emery
54   The Tree that Would Not Die,
         Dalisa Thompson
         Computer Drawing, Ginny Emery
55   The Blood that Covers Me,
         ©Mark Oliver
56   Gethsemane, Ginny Emery
         Photographs, Ginny Emery
57   The Cross, Joyce Pfitzinger
58   The Weapon of Choice, Joyce Long
59   Pencil Sketch, Ginny Emery
60   Watercolor, Ginny Emery
61   Jesus Keep Me Near the Cross,
         Laura Millirons
62   from *The Imitation of Christ*,
         Thomas à Kempis
63   Litany of the Most Precious Blood
         Design by Rosie Curtiss
64   Choices, Ginny Emery
         Photographs, Bill Emery
65   Legalism, License and Love,
         Thomas Severson
67   Washed Clean, Lori Hall
         Pencil Drawing, Abigail Apon
68   Pencil Sketch, Dee Binckley
69   He Lives!, Thomas Severson
73   Photograph, Mary Louise Storey
75   Watercolor and Computer,
         Ginny Emery
76   Photograph, Tim Fleck,
77   Just for You, Laura Millirons
78   Photo Collage, (Cheryl Garbe,
         Ginny Emery, March for Jesus)
79   We Believe, Ginny Emery
80   A Huge Lesson, C. S. Kellough
83   "Our Father," Pencil Sketch by
         Jeffrey Scott Terpstra
84   Come Unto Me, ©Pat Bailey

152

85	Pen, ink, and marker sketch, Dee Binckley	119	Immortality, Anonymous Photograph, Jane Jahnke
86	Following His Footsteps, Joyce Long	120	Significant Sacrifice, Maria Johnson
89	Photograph, Ginny Emery	121	Pencil Drawing, Janet Emery
90	Repentance, ©Pat Bailey, Photograph, Ginny Emery	122	Choose, Cassandra SeRine
		123	Sketch, Dee Binckley
91	Eyes Meet, Ginny Emery Colored Pencil Sketch, Abigail Apon	124	Altars, Ginny Emery Photograph, Ginny Emery
92	Pencil Drawing, Janet Emery	125	A Song, Cecelia Cody Photograph, Ginny Emery
93	Acceptable Sacrifice, Ginny Emery	126	Communion, Ginny Emery Photograph, Bill Emery
94	In Love, Ginny Emery		
94	Photograph, Mike Burch	127	The Goodness of God, Joyce Pfitzinger Jesus Laughing, Ralph Kozak © a colored variation of a drawing by Willis Wheatley
95	Photographs, Ginny Emery		
96	Show Us, Maria Johnson		
97	Pastel Drawing, Janet Emery		
98	Human Weakness and the Power of God, Michael Sullivant		
		128	Photograph, Bill Emery
105	Watercolor, Ginny Emery	129	Partaking Unworthily: A Communion Sermon, Ben Binckley
106	Computer Drawing, Ginny Emery		
107	Prayer, Michael Sullivant Photograph, Ginny Emery	131	Photograph, Bill Emery
		132	A Hidden Place, Ginny Emery
108	Follow the Lamb, Ginny Emery Photograph, March for Jesus, Elgin, IL	133	Charcoal Drawing, Janet Emery
		134	All I Can Do–A Song, ©Stephen Curtiss Photograph, Brad and Patti Weiss
109	Shall I be There?, Ginny Emery Photograph, Ginny Emery		
		135	Clasped Hands, Cassandra Se Rine Photograph, March for Jesus
110	More Than Life, Lori Hall		
110	Photograph, Lori Hall	136	Diligence, Cassandra Se Rine
113	My Offering, Lori Hall Photograph, Lori Hall	137	Photograph, ©Diane Wawrejko Cochrane,
114	Giver of Life, Mari Jane Wemken Photograph, Mari Jane Wemken	138	Worshipping into the Heart of God, ©Diane Wawrejko Cochrane
115	What Can I Offer?, Bob Baker, Photograph, Mari Jane Wemken	138	Line drawings, ©Diane Wawrejko Cochrane
116	His Joy, Ginny Emery and Joyce Long Photograph of Martha, Tom Adams Photograph with children, Kathleen Trock	141	Photograph, ©Diane Wawrejko Cochrane
		142	Mirror of Love, Maria Johnson
		143	Pencil Sketch, Janet Emery
		144	Colored Pencil Sketch, Jeane Heckert
117	Our Joy, Ginny Emery and Joyce Long Photograph of Grace, Tom Adams Photograph of Joshua, Jane Jahnke	145	Beloved of God, Alice Foreman
		147	Watercolor, Ginny Emery
		149	Photograph, Ginny Emery
118	Life Must Go On, Kayla Apon Pencil and Crayon drawing, Abigail Apon	150	Afterword, Thomas Severson

THE WRITERS

ABIGAIL APON
Creation   15

KAYLA APON
Life Must Go On   118

LORI APON
I'm Not Going to Cry,
    I'm Not Going to Cry!!!   26

PAT BAILEY
Come Unto Me   84
    ©used by permission
Repentance   90
    ©used by permission

BOB BAKER
What Can I Offer?   115
    ©used by permission

BEN BINCKLEY
Partaking Unworthily   129

DEE BINCKLEY
Copy of text by an unknown author
of Litany of the Most Precious
Blood from *Journal Sketchbook*   63

DIANE WAWREJKO COCHRANE
Worshipping into the Heart of God
    ©used by permission   138

CECELIA CODY
A Song   125

STEPHEN CURTISS
All I Can Do   134
    ©used by permission

GINNY EMERY
His Plan   16
In Time   25
Text   29
Prodigal's Puzzle   30
The Crucifixion   37
That Day   40
Our Prayer   45
Jesus: The Christ   46
Alone   53
Gethsemane   56
Choices   64
We Believe   79
Eyes Meet   91
Acceptable Sacrifice   93
In Love   94
Follow the Lamb   108
Shall I Be There   109
Altars   124
Communion   126
A Hidden Place   132

GINNY EMERY and JOYCE LONG
Introduction   8
His Joy   116
Our Joy   117

ALICE FORMAN
Beloved of God   145
    ©used by permission

LORI HALL
Washed Clean   67
More than Life   110
My Offering   113

MARIA JOHNSON
Show Us   96
Significant Sacrifice   120
Mirror of Love   142

C. S. KELLOUGH
Putting All our Expectancies   50
   in the Blood of the Cross
   ©used by permission
A Huge Lesson   80
   ©used by permission

THOMAS `A KEMPIS
The Imitation of Christ   62

JOYCE LONG
Divine Longing   18
The Stairport   32
The Weapon of Choice   58
Following in His Footsteps   86

LAURA MILLIRON
The Only Hope I Have   22
Jesus, Keep me Near the Cross   61
Just For You   77

ROSS NELSON
My God, My God   49
   Why Have You Forsaken Me?

MARK OLIVER
The Blood that Covers Me: A Song   55
   ©used by permission

JOYCE PFITZINGER
The Cross   57
The Goodness of God   127

CASSANDRA SERINE
Choose   122
Claspéd Hands   135
Diligence   136

TOM SEVERSON
Foreword   11
Legalism, License, and Love   65
He Lives   69
Afterword   150

N. J. SUIRE
His Obedience   42

MICHAEL SULLIVANT
Human Weakness and the   98
   Power of God ©used by permission
Prayer ©used by permission   107

MARCIA THOMAS
This Pain   52

DELISA THOMPSON
The Tree That Would Not Die   54

MARI JANE WEMKEN
Giver of Life   114

OUR GRATITUDE TO:
An Anonymous Author:
   Immortality   119
The unknown writer of
   Litany of the Most
   Precious Blood, Brugge, Flanders   63

THE ARTISTS

TOM ADAMS
Photographs:
  Grace   117
  Martha   116

ABIGAIL APON
Pencil drawing   67
Colored Pencil drawing   91
Pencil and crayon drawing   118

DEE BINCKLEY
Journal Sketchbook pages:
  Devalued   68
  The Risen Christ   85
  What is the Human Face of God?   123

MIKE BURCH
Photograph   94

DIANE WAWREJKO COCHRANE
Photographs:
  Diane ©Used by permission.   137
  Diane Aloft ©Used by permission.   141
  Line drawings ©Used by permission. 138-9

ROSIE CURTISS
Design for Litany
  of the Most Precious Blood   63

GINNY EMERY
Photographs:
  Sky, Korean Mountains   16
  Sky, Albanian Mountains   17
  Near the Damascus Gate   21
  Auto graveyard near Durres   30
  Broken pottery   30
  Man along the road   30
  Kenora Road   31
  Pottery   35
  McHenry County Spring   53

  Gethsemane   56
  Holocaust Memorial   56
  Collage of Faces   78
  (with photographs from Ginny
  Emery, Cheryl Garbe and Elgin,
  Illinois March for Jesus)
  Path   89
  Iron Grate   90
  Fred   95
  Marie   95
  Earthenware oil jars   107
  Moravian Lamb   109
  Cross at VCF   124
  Feast in Tirana   125
  Rose   149
Pencil sketch:
  A Sword
Watercolors:
  Stairway to Heaven   33
  Behind Many Crosses   36
  Red and Yellow Cross   38
  Dark Crucifixion   48
  Cross upon Cross   49
  Yellow Cross   60
  Swirling Cross   75
  Wave   105
  Butterfly   147
Computer drawings:
  Simple Reality   54
  Brown Jug   106

JANET EMERY
Cover
Computer drawing:
  Troubled Waters   28-29
Pastel:
  A Reflection of Your Son   97
Charcoal drawing   133
Pencil drawings:
  Repetition of Cover   10
  Segment from Self-portraits   52
  Set Free   92-93
  Angel with one
    of the Ten Virgins   121
  Hand   143

WILLIAM EMERY
Photographs:
  Sticks in Water   13
  Two Wine Glasses   64
  Pouring Wine   126
  Bread and Wine   128
  Bread   131

TIM FLECK
Photograph   76

COREY HAGBERG
Oil painting   24-25

LORI HALL
Photographs:
  Rebecca   110
  Rebecca as an Infant   113

JEANE HECKERT
Colored Pencil:
  Rainbow Cross   144

JANE JAHNKE
Photographs:
  Joshua and Bea   119
  Joshua   117

RALPH KOZAK
Screen Print:
  Jesus Laughing: A colored   127
  Variation of Willis Wheatley's
  drawing
    ©Used by Permission

MARCH FOR JESUS-ELGIN, IL
Photographs:
  Two Flags   108
  Clasped hands   135

DAVID ROY
Pencil Sketch:
  Centurion at the Crucifixion,   41
    Courtesy of Dale Jaacks

MARY LOUISE STOREY
Photograph   73

JEFFREY SCOTT TERPSTRA
Pencil Sketch:
  Our Father
    Used by permission.   83

KATHLEEN TROCK
Photograph   116

JOHAN VANDER TOL
Pencil and Pastel:
  Abstract with Hand   46
  Abstract with Face and Form   47

BRAD AND PATTI WEISS
Photographs:
  Grand Canyon   14
  Florida   134

MARI JANE WEMKEN
Photographs:
  Girls Dance Team   114
  At Sunday Worship   115

UNKNOWN ARTISTS
Watercolor:
  Segment of Sheep and Shepherd   39

RESOURCES

BOOKS

Heart Songs, a collection of poems by Pat Bailey
    Pat Bailey
    39W543 Seavy Road; Batavia, Illinois 60510

From Stumbling to Perfecting,
    a book of teaching on the crucified life by
    C.S. Kellough
    Builders Inc.
    P. O. Box 55924; Indianapolis, Indiana 46205

DANCE

Dances Wawrejko:
    Lectures, Performances, Workshops, and Choreography
    Dances Wawrejko
    1302 Wakeman; Wheaton, Illinois 60187

MUSIC

Worship Music by Bob Baker and Steve Curtiss
    Wellspring Music
    P.O. Box 523; Elgin, Illinois 60121
    http//www.wellspringworship.com

Worship Music by Mark Oliver
    Mighty Warrior Music International
    9001 Rt. 176; Crystal Lake, IL 60014
    http//www.mwmi.org

PREACHING AND TEACHING

Cassette tapes by Tom Severson
    Vineyard Christian Fellowship
    205 Fulton Street; Elgin, Illinois 60120
    847-697-8001

Cassette tapes by Michael Sullivant
    Abounding Grace Bookstore
    11610 Grandview Road; Kansas City, Missouri 664137
    http//www.agbmcgf.com
    1-800-552-2449

PRINTING

    Print Systems, Inc.
    2261 East Beltline NE; Grand Rapids, Michigan 49525
    616-361-6333; Fax: 616-361-2064

PUBLISHERS
Meet Me at the Cross
Churches and organizations can ask for special purchasing information for evangelism, education or fundraising.
Given Word Publishers, Inc.
P. O. Box 425; Crystal Lake, Illinois 60039-0425
Fax: 815-356-7410

REPRODUCTIONS OF ARTWORK
Abstracts by Johan Vander Tol
Our Father by Jeffrey Scott Terpstra
Master's Prints
P. O. Box 1015; Jenison, Michigan 49429
616-457-7541

Meet Me at the Cross, Illustrations from selected pages
Given Word Publishers
P. O. Box 425; Crystal Lake, Illinois 60039
Fax: 815-356-7410

OTHER
Prayer Ministry of Alice Foreman, author of "Beloved of God"
Kingdom Builders
P. O. Box 4142; Cleveland, Tennessee 37320